# GLOBETROTTER™

## *Travel Guide*

# VIENNA

PAUL

NEW
HOLLAND

NEW
HOLLAND

*** Highly recommended
** Recommended
* See if you can

First edition published in 2008
by New Holland Publishers (UK) Ltd
London • Cape Town • Sydney • Auckland
10 9 8 7 6 5 4 3 2 1
website: www.newhollandpublishers.com

Garfield House, 86 Edgware Road
London W2 2EA,
United Kingdom

80 McKenzie Street
Cape Town 8001,
South Africa

Unit 1, 66 Gibbes Street,
Chatswood, NSW 2067,
Australia

218 Lake Road,
Northcote, Auckland,
New Zealand

Distributed in the USA by
The Globe Pequot Press, Connecticut

ISBN 978 1 84537 968 1

This guidebook has been written by independent
authors and updaters. The information therein represents
their impartial opinion, and neither they nor the
publishers accept payment in return for including in the
book or writing more favourable reviews of any of the
establishments. Whilst every effort has been made to
ensure that this guidebook is as accurate and up to
date as possible, please be aware that the facts quoted
are subject to change, particularly the price of food,
transport and accommodation. The Publisher accepts no
responsibility or liability for any loss, injury or inconve-
nience incurred by readers or travellers using this guide.

**Keep us Current**
Information in travel guides is apt to change, which is
why we regularly update our guides. We'd be grateful to
receive feedback if you've noted something we should
include in our updates. If you have new information,
please share it with us by writing to the Publishing
Manager, Globetrotter, at the office nearest to you
(addresses on this page). The most significant
contribution to each new edition will receive a free
copy of the updated guide.

**Publishing Manager:** Thea Grobbelaar
**DTP Cartographic Manager:** Genené Hart
**Editor:** Nicky Steenkamp
**Design and DTP:** Nicole Bannister
**Cartographers:** Genené Hart and Lauren Fick
**Picture Researcher:** Zainoenisa Manuel
**Consultants:** Mathias Kleemann and Carole French
**Proofreader:** Mariëlle Renssen
Reproduction by Resolution, Cape Town
Printed and bound by Times Offset (M) Sdn. Bhd., Malaysia

**Photographic Credits:**
**Caroline Jones:** page 73; **David Bowden:** pages 30, 91;
F1 Online/Photo Access: page 82; **Fantuz
Olimpio/Sime/Photo Access:** page 26; **Fresh Food
Images/Photo Access:** page 29; **Imagebroker/Photo
Access:** page 70; **Imagestate/Photo Access:** pages 111;
**International PhotoBank:** pages 4, 27, 47, 76, 87;
**Jon Smith:** pages 13, 23, 35, 37, 39, 51, 52, 54, 55, 56,
59, 60, 62, 67, 75, 112; **Neil Setchfield:** title page;
**Paul Tingay:** pages 7, 16, 18, 19, 21, 31, 32, 36, 40, 41,
42, 44, 50, 61, 65, 66, 68, 72, 80, 81, 85, 88, 89, 90,
94, 96, 97, 98, 101, 103, 105, 109; **Pictures Colour
Library:** front cover, pages 8, 106, 110; **Robin McKelvie:**
page 25; **Sime/Photo Access:** pages 15, 38, 43, 48, 71,
79, 104; **Travel Pix Collection/jonarnoldimages.com:**
page 92; **Walter Bibikow/jonarnoldimages.com:** page
11; **Westend 61/Photo Access:** page 53

**Acknowledgements**
The publishers and author would like to thank Andrew
and Louise Brooke, Jimmy and Gillian Girdlestone,
Clare, Anthony, Dom Alexander and Ann of the
Danube. Also, Prof. Kees Pouderoijen and Florian Auer
for their silverwit Dutch and Austrian company, and
particularly Romy Kleemann and Mathias Kleemann of
Vienna for their constant assistance, advice and humour.

**Cover:** *The Museum of Fine Arts.*
**Title page:** *Mozart souvenirs at a Vienna gift shop.*

# CONTENTS

# 1
# Introducing
# Vienna

Across the street a music student plays a Mozart serenade, violin case for coins at her formal skirt. In the spring sunshine, the sidewalk café is already busy. A fresh rose on each table, waiters in white shirts, black ties. An open *fiaker* hackney trots past. A young mum pushes twins in their pram as a chimney sweep in traditional bell-hop cap parks his Harley. Above the passers-by gleams the copper-green dome of St Michael, guardian gate into the Imperial Palace. There is the aroma of freshly ground coffee, cinnamon-hint strudel, crispy Kaiser-semmel rolls, Sachertorte with cream, the snap of newspapers, the buzz of conversation. *Grüss Gott*. Welcome to Vienna.

## THE LAND

Vienna is the **capital of Austria**, in central Europe. The country covers an area of 83,855km² (32,368 sq miles), roughly the size of Scotland. Although much of it is winelands, fruit farms, forest and skiing alps, 70% of the Austrian population are city dwellers.

The city spreads in a horseshoe shape back from the **Danube** and its fringing slopes of grapevines to the **Wienerwald**, the Vienna Woods, inspiration to music maestros Beethoven, Mozart and Schubert. The Danube to the east has been artificially divided into four rivers to prevent flooding. Vienna is where **Mozart** wrote Eine kleine Nachtmusik, where **Strauss** invented the waltz (a less than refined gallop in its time), where **Beethoven**'s brilliance shone like the stars and where **Schubert** penned 600 lieder (songs).

**TOP ATTRACTIONS**

*** **Hofburg Imperial Palace**: Vienna Boys' Choir and Spanish Riding School.
*** **Inner city**: cobblestones, markets, hackney cabs and Holocaust memorial.
*** **Danube boat trip to Melk monastery**: tiny village, mountain castles, gardens and awesome Baroque monastery.
** **Kunsthistorisches Museum**: world's fourth largest collection of fine art.
** **Schloss Schönbrunn**: gardens, palace, grand sculptures and beautiful views.
** **Stephansdom**: climb the spire for views of Vienna.

**Opposite:** *Mozart statue in the Burggarten in Vienna.*

## FACT FILE

• Vienna ranks tenth in world tourism statistics (France is number one).
• Every second Viennese owns a car.
• Richard the Lionheart was kidnapped in 1192 and held to ransom in Dürnstein mountain castle on the Danube.
• Vienna has at least 12 breads including box-shaped Finnebrot, plaited sweet striezel and pumpkin-seeded kürbiskernbrot. The croissant was invented in Vienna.
• Beethoven lived at 67 residences in Vienna between 1792, when he was 22, and 1827, when he died.
• Franz Schubert, Anton Bruckner, Beethoven, Gluck, Brahms, Hugo Wolf, Lanner and the whole musical Strauss family are buried in Vienna's central cemetery.

## The Old City

The historic and once-walled centre of Vienna is a walking city. If you are map-wise and don't pause too long to admire the awesome plethora of museums, churches, squares and old-world cafés, you can stroll its 2km (1.6 miles) north to south, or east to west in under three hours. But you won't. There is simply too much to see: the ethereal clouds, cupids, saints and nymphs in Baroque churches, the prancing white horses of the Spanish Riding School, the Vienna Boys' Choir (there are four choirs, incidentally), *fiaker* hackney cabs and twisty cobbled alleyways.

Vienna's ancient inner city has seen the **Roman** legions come and go, provided a home to practically every musical genius in the western world and by dint of war, diplomacy and above all astute marriage manoeuvring, allowed one family, the **Habsburg** dynasty (15th–20th century), to rule half of Europe for 640 years.

Until the mid-19th century, Vienna was a medieval walled city, trading crossroads of the Holy Roman Empire and autocratic ruler of 50 million people. It was

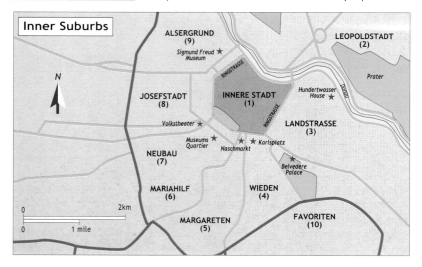

Inner Suburbs

N

0 _____ 2km
0 _____ 1 mile

ALSERGRUND (9)
Sigmund Freud ★ Museum
LEOPOLDSTADT (2)
Prater
JOSEFSTADT (8)
INNERE STADT (1)
Hundertwasser House ★
Volkstheater ★
LANDSTRASSE (3)
Museums ★ Quartier
★ ★ Karlsplatz
Naschmarkt
NEUBAU (7)
Belvedere Palace
MARIAHILF (6)
WIEDEN (4)
MARGARETEN (5)
FAVORITEN (10)
RINGSTRASSE

also coveted by Hungarians, Swedes, Russians, Napoleon and always the dreaded Turks to the east. It was here, too, 100 years ago that the psychotic, young, and unhappy **Hitler** came to try his artistic talent. Unfortunately he was too unknown then for Vienna's **Sigmund Freud**, inventor of psychoanalysis, to plumb the dark dreaming of his fevered brain.

**Above:** *Kaiser Franz Josef and his wife Sisi.*

## The Ringstrasse

In 1857 **Kaiser Franz Josef** decided old Vienna was getting too big for its venerable boots, the crumbling walls and battlements getting in the way of Imperial expansion. If Paris could have its Champs Elysées and Berlin the Brandenburg Gate, why not Vienna?

Down went the old walls and up went the twin-spired Gothic church (Votivkirche), the new town hall, gardens, theatre, neo-Renaissance parliament, university, opera and, just in case, two new barracks. For himself, the emperor also built a little extension to his **Hofburg Palace** in the Inner City. All are linked by a grand circular boulevard, the **Ringstrasse**.

## The Inner Suburbs

Between the Ringstrasse and another circular boulevard, the Gürtel, lie Vienna's inner suburbs, numbered by district (*see* panel). These include Alsergrund (where Sigmund Freud's house is situated); Mariahilf (Mary's Help, location of the Naschmarkt); Landstrasse (here you'll find Hundertwasser House and village – where even the loo is called The Toilet of Modern Art – and Prince Eugène of Savoy's palace and gardens, Belvedere); Wieden (with Karlsplatz Church, Vienna's grandest Baroque masterpiece); and Neubau (location of the Volkstheater and the sprawling Museums Quartier).

---

**TIDILY PACKAGED**

Vienna is divided into 23 districts or *Bezirke*.

The Innere Stadt (No. 1) has the Stephansdom, Hofburg and Ringstrasse, Leopoldstadt (2) the Prater Ferris wheel, Augarten, the Flak Towers and the Blue Danube. The Belvedere Palace and Gardens are in Landstrasse (3), as is Mozart's grave in St Marx Cemetery. Karlskirche's gorgeous church is in Wieden (4) and next door in Margareten (5) is The Third Man Museum. The colourful Naschmarkt is in Mariahilf (No. 6), while the Museums Quartier is on the edge of the Ringstrasse and Neubau (7). Josefstadt (No. 8) has the Rathaus, and Alsergrund (9) the Liechtenstein Museum. Schönbrunn Palace is in Heitzing, number 13.

**Right:** *The Volkstheater, or People's Theatre, looks over the busy Museums Quartier.*

### ON YOUR BIKE

Vienna has nearly 800km (497 miles) of cycling paths. You can go right around the Ringstrasse of gorgeous buildings (Rathaus, Landtmann Café, Burgtheater, Parliament) on a bike. Get information and a map of all the cycle paths from www.wien.at You can take your bike on the U-Bahn carriages with a bicycle symbol and on trains marked with a bicycle logo on the timetable. Opening times for bikes on the U-Bahn carriages and trains are: Monday–Friday 09:00–15:00 and after 18:30. Open all day from 09:00 on Saturday and Sunday. No bikes on buses and only folding bikes on trains. Lots of cycle-hire stations e.g. Citybike, tel: 0810 500 500 or www.citybikewien.at

## Blue Danube

Waltz maestro Johann Strauss's Schönen Blauen Donau (Beautiful Blue Danube) rises in Germany's Black Forest and, like the dance, the river twists and twirls ever faster as it flows east through country after country to the Black Sea 2859km (1776 miles) away.

Vienna's Danube consists of four waterways dredged, embanked and tamed. There are some 15 bridges across the Danube Canal, which separates the Inner City and suburbs from the huge 'island' of Leopoldstadt with its Prater funfair, an area 15 times the size of the Inner City. Donau City, UNO City (a complex of UN skyscrapers) and the ethnic riverside cafés of Copa Kagrana lie across the Reichs bridge along the Neue Donau (New Danube), as does the pleasant Donau Park (you can't miss the radio tower). Lovely water gardens lie on the northeast bank of the Alte Donau (Old Danube), itself divided into the Upper and Lower Old Danube.

## The Outer Suburbs

The outer suburbs are often hill-sloping winelands or fruit farms on the edge of the Vienna Woods. They include the **Tiergarten** public park, the former hunting preserve of the Imperial family which boasts wolf, wild boar, buck and red squirrels.

The southernmost suburbs feature the Imperial **Schönbrunn** (beautiful fountain) palace and gardens. The palace has 1500 rooms. The Augarten is another of Vienna's many green parks. Apart from the delicate porcelain sold in the park, there are two monstrous concrete anti-aircraft towers or *Flaktürme* built by the Nazis to ward off attack. The walls are 5m (16ft) thick.

The **Zentralfriedhof** (Central Cemetery) in Simmering is where 3 million people are buried, including Beethoven, Schubert, Brahms and the Strauss family. A million Viennese arrive on All Saints' Day, 1 November, each year to light little candles inside red lanterns on the 300,000 graves.

## Vienna Woods

The **Wienerwald** is a great arc of forested hills and meadows on the edge of the city's suburbs. It stretches from the Danube Valley in the north to the foothills of the Austrian Alps in the south. It is a huge, hilly, untouched and heavily forested area of 1250km$^2$ (483 sq miles) with hideaway cycling tracks and tiny villages. It has always been the Viennese R'n'R area with families sometimes spending all summer in the bracing wilderness. There are 40 mountain-biking trails, always a little restaurant around the next corner, view points, small lakes, rivers, toboggan runs and even a few humble skiing slopes.

---

### TO MARKET, TO MARKET

Travelling by tram, or just walking, you will inevitably come across a mid-week or Saturday market. There is the Friday and Saturday Organic Market in Freyung in the Innere Stadt, and the flea market or *Flohmarkt* on Saturdays at Kettenbrückengasse 5 with colourful traders from every part of Europe. The Brunnenmarkt at 16 Brunnengasse stretches for a kilometre and is open Monday–Saturday. The Art and Crafts *Kunstmarkt* is held in a monastic courtyard at 1 Heiligenkreuzerhof from April to September, but only on the first weekend of the month. The largest of them all is the Naschmarkt, a Vienna phenomenon of fruit, vegetables, spices and restaurants. From mid-November onwards there are child Jesus, or *Christkindlmärkte*, at the Rathaus, Karlsplatz, Schönbrunn, and Spittelberg, with much joviality and *glühwein*.

## Climate

Vienna has a mild climate by European standards, but it can be hot in summer and cold in winter. Showers are frequent in summer, and winter winds off the Hungarian Steppe exacerbate the chill factor. The mean temperature in July is 19°C (66°F), and January can be freezing. Vienna is much drier than, for example, London.

## HISTORY IN BRIEF
### The Celts

The Celts, an Indo-European people whose language is still spoken in Ireland today, had settled in the Danube valley in the Vienna area by 1000BC. They are also known as the Hallstatt folk after an Austrian village where bronze and iron artefacts were excavated. Their decorative art probably makes them Vienna's first artists. That apart, the Celts were a pesky crowd. They introduced the short fighting sword to the Romans and on one occasion even had the nerve to attack and sack Rome.

### Romans on the Rampage

In AD433 Vienna, known as **Vindobona**, was an outpost of Roman Carnuntum, Province of Pannonia Superior, and under attack by relentless Mongols, Goths, Huns and Vandals.

The Romans left us a magnificent legacy of language, law and architecture. But they were also fond of slavery and crucifying those they did not like, on occasion 2000 at a time. They certainly slaughtered the Celts. The trouble was the Danube. Among other advantages the river offered, it was the crossroads of the Polish amber trade, that mesmerizing yellow-brown fossil resin from coniferous trees, used in Roman jewellery and much prized.

So in 16BC, the Romans poured over the Celtic alpine kingdom of Noricum and, as at the Rhine, established a line of forts along the Danube which they called 'frontier limits' or Limes, the main camp being Carnuntum with Vindobona, now Vienna, as an auxiliary. Civilians were encouraged to settle around the Roman Forum, now Vienna's **Hoher Markt** (High Market Square).

**Left:** *The renovated multi-patterned roof of Stephansdom includes the Austrian and Habsburg eagles.*

## Charlemagne

The **Dark Ages** (AD500–1000) became less dark once super-warrior **Charlemagne** bashed a few heads together, founded the Holy Roman Empire, encouraged all to read (even if he couldn't himself), and soon everyone began building those soaring Gothic churches of which **Stephansdom** (St Stephen's Cathedral) in Vienna is a beautiful example.

The history of Europe is largely one of tribal warfare: for land, trade, power and women. Charlemagne meantime followed the Roman example and established the Eastern Frontier, or Ostmark, along the Danube in the

---

**LUCKY SOOTY**

In medieval Vienna, an era of wooden houses, to not clean your chimney could bring the death penalty. So a visit by the chimney sweep with his white cap was always a great relief, especially as it was believed his sooty countenance would ward off the devil and his attendant evils, such as disease. Even today, if you see a lucky chimney sweep in the morning, you'll have good luck for the rest of the day. So the Viennese say.

**Opposite:** *High Altar*
*inside Stephansdom.*

9th century. Vienna (or Wenia from the Illyro-Celtic *verdunja*) was first mentioned in writing in 881. It means a forest stream. The small 'Wien' river still runs to the southeast of the city, though largely underground. A hundred years later, in 996, the Ostmark was being referred to as Ostarrîchi, Österreich (Austria) in today's German.

This post-Roman classical period saw the migration of religions. Catholic Christianity became dominant in Western Europe and German-speaking people, particularly Charlemagne's **Franks** (hence France and Frankfurt), spread their Germanic language throughout Europe even as far as Britain.

## HISTORICAL CALENDAR

**500BC** Vienna area occupied by Celtic-speaking clans. They named it Vindobona.
**AD12** The civil settlement at Vindobona (Vienna) becomes a military fort under the Roman 10th Legion.
**AD433** Romans abandon area to invading German-speaking tribes. Vienna remains a crossroads of peoples and trade during the 'Dark Ages'.
**AD800** Charlemagne crowned Holy Roman Emperor. Vienna area is part of his Ostmark military colony.
**AD881** Wenia name first appears in a written document.
**AD976** The Babenberg dynasty acquire the Ostmark and rule Ostarrîchi for 270 years.
**AD996** A Latin parchment mentions the name Ostarrîchi for the first time. Cathedrals, crusades and water mills are invented. This era is later

called the 'Middle Ages'.
**1273** Rudolf becomes the first Habsburg to be Holy Roman Emperor.
**1420–21** Wiener Geserah; pogrom against the Jews.
**1454** Johann Gutenberg invents the printing press. Italian Renaissance, Albrecht Dürer's art, secular Meistersinger music.
**1529** First Turkish siege of Vienna (1500 Viennese killed). Spread of Reformation Lutherism.
**1679** Some 70,000 Viennese die in the plague.
**1683** Second Turkish Siege. Age of Baroque. Copernicus confirms the earth revolves around the sun. Isaac Newton invents Calculus.
**1740–80** Maria Theresia is the first female emperor.
**1805** and **1809** Napoleon occupies Vienna following the French Revolution.
**1848** Unsuccessful revolutions throughout

Europe.
**1857** Kaiser Franz Josef I launches the Ringstrasse building project.
**1870** Vienna gets its first trams. The automobile is invented in **1885**, the first movie in **1895**.
**1914** Franz Ferdinand, heir to the throne of Austria, is assassinated. Leads to World War I which eventually leaves Austria without an empire.
**1919** Social Democrats win control of Vienna City Council. Red Vienna.
**1938** Hitler's Anschluss takeover of Austria.
**1939–45** World War II. Austrian youth conscripted into German army.
**1945–55** USA, Britain, France and Russia occupy post-war Vienna.
**1955** Austria retrieves its independence.
**1981** Vienna becomes the third location of UNO.
**1995** Austria joins the EU.

## Cathedral and Crusade

The Saxon king, **Otto the Great** (these titles were a sort of honours list of the day), gave the Ostmark, the eastern military colony, to the **Babenberg** clan in 976, with instructions to hold it against the Hungarian Magyars. Conscripting serfs and shoemakers, farmers and monks, the Babenbergs inched down the Danube from their fortified Melk monastery and eventually took Vienna. One Babenberg, **Leopold III**, even managed to become the patron saint of Austria.

In 1147, a church where Stephansdom stands today was completed in Vienna's Innere Stadt. Stephan, the first Christian martyr stoned to death (in Palestine) around AD35, is a popular boys' name in both Austria and Hungary. Building in stone and particularly the distribution of weights and arches were techniques borrowed from the expanding Arab empire which would soon threaten Vienna. This period was known as the **Middle Ages**. To the Italian Renaissance folk, the new cathedrals that had blossomed throughout Europe were 'Gothic'– creations of the dreadful civilization-destroying Goths, or Germans.

**Islam**, meanwhile, fired by the prophet Muhammad's supremely poetic Qur'an, had conquered the Middle East and much of the Mediterranean. Catholic Christians, cross in one hand, sword in the other, were determined to rescue the Holy Places where Jesus had lived. So they set out on a series of **crusades**. Those along the route had their castles trashed, cities razed and women raped. Confusing pillage for sanctity, second sons got rich. But not many souls were saved. Nor did they hang onto Jerusalem for long.

**Richard the Lionheart**, King of England, shipwrecked and forced to go overland, stopped over in Vienna in 1192 on his way back from Palestine. Recognized, he was kidnapped, having apparently insulted Babenberg Duke **Leopold V** and the Emperor during the Siege of Acre. He was imprisoned in **Dürnstein**

## PRAISE THE LORD

There are Anglican, Baptist, United Methodist, Orthodox, Buddhist, Russian, Greek and Islamic places of worship in Vienna, plus 660 Catholic churches. The Jewish City Synagogue is near the Bermuda Triangle. As a security measure bring your passport. Many churches have music on offer during services, e.g. the Vienna Boys' Choir (though not July to mid-September) and Gregorian Plain Chant at the 09:15 Mass at the Burgkapelle in the old city. There are always tickets left that you can queue for.

mountaintop castle on the Danube until, in true warrior baron style, a huge ransom was paid. The ruins of the castle are still there.

## Toiling Tillers

Progress helped to change European and Viennese society. However, poor harvests created homeless people. Then came bubonic plague, or the **Black Death**, which, because of the appallingly overcrowded and hygiene-starved conditions in which people lived, wiped out a third of Vienna's (and Austria's) population between 1300 and 1500.

There were regular peasant revolts and increasing numbers of people moved into Vienna. Women married at 16, men usually 10 years later. The nuclear family unit of mother, father and children solidified, but many cities had to establish brothels to contain male violence.

## Habsburgs of Hofburg

Although it was the opportunist **Ottokar II** of Bohemia who started building the **Hofburg** (see page 45), initially a rough fort, it was the **Habsburgs** who turned Vienna into what it is today. The remote castle of Habichtsberg overlooking the River Reuss in today's Switzerland was the Habsburg's ancestral *schloss*. **Rudolf of Habsburg**, the German King, killed Ottokar in battle. His family then ruled Austria, from Vienna, for the next 640 years until Austria was defeated in **World War I**. The family also held on to the title of Holy Roman Emperor from 1440 until forced by Napoleon to abandon it in 1806.

## Renaissance Man

Renaissance Italian man saw himself as the born-again enlightened purveyor of classical scholarship, science, geographical discovery, culture and the arts. And what with Donatello, Machiavelli, Brunelleschi, Leonardo da Vinci, Michelangelo and Bellini, they did just that. Everybody copied them, not least Vienna. The Habsburgs' main pursuit, however, was to guarantee

their dynasty by adroit marriage diplomacy. While others made war, happy Vienna made judicious nuptials. At a more human level, this was also the era of the increasingly secular Minnesänger, Fastnachtspiele plays, Schwank fables, comic tales and the Dr Faustus drama. It was also the time of Albrecht Dürer, whose graphic artistry can be seen in the **Albertina Museum** in Vienna.

## The Turks are Coming

The population of the Holy Roman Empire at this time was about 8 million. It included the Netherlands, Germany, Switzerland and half of Italy. Transparent glass had just been invented, as had the new WC toilet.

To the **Islamic Ottomans** or 'people of the east' the wealthy city of Vienna was tempting; city of the 'golden apple' they called it. Europe was conveniently divided along religious lines: Catholic, Protestant, Reformation, Counter-Reformation, Lutherans, Jesuits. And the infidels had brought back to Vienna extraordinary delicacies from the new world of the Americas (tobacco, potatoes, tomatoes and maize – not to mention the gold and silver of Moctezuma), revolutionizing Europe's eating habits and lifestyle.

The Turks had captured Constantinople (Istanbul), capital of the Byzantine eastern Christian empire, in 1453 and by 1521 these ferocious horsemen were on

**Above:** *Albertina Museum has drawings by Rembrandt, Raphael and Michelangelo.*

### ALFRED REDL

It was 05:55 on 24 May 1913 when one Nizetas collected a letter from the main post office in Vienna. It was a letter with instructions and money from the Russian secret service. And the Austrian spooks knew it. They had set a trap. Nizetas was in fact Alfred Redl, colonel and head of the Imperial Austrian army's counterespionage service. He was homosexual and had been blackmailed. Chased through the Innere Stadt, he was caught, handed a pistol and told to do what officers and gentlemen did. He shot himself. All very discreet... But journalist Egon Kisch broke the juicy homosexuality and espionage bits and became a tabloid hero.

the move again. Serbia fell, Hungary was overrun, and a Habsburg army was defeated at the battle of Mohács in 1526. Three years later, on 27 September 1529, the Turks were at the rather dilapidated gates of Vienna with their state-of-the-art firearms, infantry and artillery.

## Cannon and Scimitar

The first siege only lasted three weeks. Vienna's rundown walls and small garrison under Count Salm fought bravely in spite of 1500 Viennese dying in the shelling. The early onset of winter may have dissuaded the Turks, or perhaps their defeat of Hungary was enough for them for the moment. Anyway, the Turks sloped off, leaving Vienna to build decent star-shaped fortifications that would last until 1857. They left a calling card: in 1555, **coffee** was introduced into the Empire.

The sporadic conflict down the centuries between these two cultural hegemonies, Islam and Christianity, has of course lasted until this day, albeit the suicide bomber is a new feature.

## Religion, Politics and War

Politics, money and the delights of the flesh have occupied the Viennese as much as any people. But in Vienna, religious argument always seemed more important. Soon after revolutionary reformer **Martin Luther** dramatically arrived on the scene, nationalism, politics, economics, social justice, religious schism and war became inextricably entwined. The birth of Protestantism and the Catholic church's counter to it was to trouble Europe for the next four centuries, with

Vienna – being capital of the Holy Roman Empire – often the epicentre.

It was not long before 80% of Viennese were Protestant; Protestantism was particularly appealing to women, apparently. So the Emperor called in the 'dogs of the papacy', the **Jesuits**, to set things right. It all developed into the awful Europe-wide 30 years' (1618–48) war. Disaster replaced prosperity as the four horsemen of the apocalypse stalked the land. As if that was not enough, back came the **Turks** and a second siege in 1683. This time, it lasted for 62 days. Only the combined imperial and winged cavalry of the Polish forces managed to lift the siege. Defeated Grand Vizier **Kara Mustafa** – as custom dictated – had one of his men strangle him with a silken cord.

## The Baroque Age

Every ceiling, cupola, corner, wall and interior surface packed with marble columns, gilt twirls, pastel saints, cherubs, puff pastry clouds in a phantasmagoria of ornamentation is one way of describing the **Baroque** style which took Vienna's rich and religious by storm in the 17th and 18th centuries. The word Baroque comes from that for the rough or imperfectly shaped pearl, and covers a flourishing mixture of classical architecture, drama, literature, music and the visual arts. The colours are gorgeous, the gilt awesome and the attention to detail staggering; it is rather like repeatedly walking into a series of Aladdin caves in its freedom of form, motion and feeling. The absolute monarchs of Europe, including the Habsburgs, adored it and tried very hard to convert every church and palace into the new style.

The age of Copernicus, calculus, printing press and new world discovery arrived. Better agricultural techniques prompted an agricultural revolution but also migration to the cities and the start of industrialization. In the German-speaking lands of the Empire, Goethe's blood and thunder had to compete with recently invented popular novels.

**Opposite:** *Master crafts-man Anton Pilgram's 1513 self-sculpture in Stephansdom.*

## MUSIC MAESTRO

The music greats of Vienna
include the following:
**Beethoven, Ludwig van**.
1770–1827. Composer, e.g.
Emperor Concerto.
**Brahms, Johannes**.
1833–97. Composer,
e.g. Violin Concerto.
**Brückner, Anton**. 1824–96.
Organist and composer, e.g.
Romantic Symphony.
**Haydn, Josef**. 1732–1809.
Composer, e.g. Gypsy Rondo.
**Karas, Anton**. 1906–85.
Zither music for *The Third
Man* movie.
**Liszt, Franz**. 1811–86.
Piano virtuoso and composer,
e.g. Hungarian Rhapsody.
**Mahler, Gustav**. 1860–1911.
Composer, e.g. Titan
Symphony.
**Mozart, Wolfgang Amadeus**.
1756–91. Composer, e.g.
Symphony No. 40 in G minor.
**Schubert, Franz Peter**. 1797–
1828. Composed 600 lieder.
**Strauss, Johann, Jr**. 1825–99.
Waltz King, e.g. Blue Danube.
**Wolf, Hugo**. 1860–1903.
Composer of lieder.

## Maria Theresia

In 1740, Maria Theresia became the Habsburg Kaiserina.
This caused considerable unease among every full-
blooded male monarch from Spain to Bavaria. Over the
next 40 years she fought the Prussians, the French and
the Russians, directing armies and diplomacy from her
palace at **Schönbrunn**. Like Elizabeth I of England she
was known as the 'Virgin Empress' – in fact she had 16
children. Her husband was a bit of a rake, actually, so
she set up the **Chastity Commission** in 1747. Actresses,
those favourites of royalty, were specifically targeted.
She was rabidly anti-Protestant, anti-Semitic and became
incredibly obese in old age. But she did introduce state
education for both men and women.

## Napoleon Bonaparte

**Marie Antoinette**, daughter of Maria Theresia and wife
of the King of France, was guillotined in 1793 during
the French Revolution. For the next 22 years Europe
was in turmoil as Napoleon Bonaparte sought to con-
quer and anchor the revolution.

Napoleon's highly motivated and experienced
armies conquered most of Europe, occupying Vienna in
1805 and again in 1809. He rather fancied himself as
the new Holy Roman Emperor, but eventually the
British and Prussians defeated him. The victorious
powers met at the **Congress of Vienna** in 1815.

## Affairs of State

Europe's elite flocked to
Vienna, to horse-trade,
debate and carve up
Europe. But it was not
only maps, committees
and treaties. It was also a
nine-month social extra-
vaganza of sumptuous
dinners, balls, waltzes,
soireés, and divertisse-
ments. Everyone spoke

THEODOR-HERZL-STIEGE

DR. THEODOR HERZL (1860-1904)
SCHRIFTSTELLER UND JOURNALIST
ER SCHRIEB 1896 IN WIEN DAS BUCH
„DER JUDENSTAAT"
UND GAB DAMIT DIE KÜHNE IDEE
ZUR GRÜNDUNG DES STAATES ISRAEL

GEWIDMET 1996 VOM KULTURVEREIN WIEN INNERE STADT

**Left:** *A plaque commemorating Theodor Herzl's book, which led to the creation of Israel.*
**Opposite:** *Beethoven and Mozart meet.*

French at that time. It was the world's first summit (*see* panel, page 16), popular among nations ever since. Europe's monarchs, to their considerable relief, regained their crowns and turned the clock back. But revolution, boosted by industrialization, was in the air.

### Revolution

The failure of the potato and wheat crops in Europe sparked revolution in 1848. It spread like wildfire from Paris. Only the Netherlands, Belgium and Britain (which had more liberal forms of government) escaped the flames. It was ruthlessly crushed in Vienna by **Kaiser Franz Josef I** (1848–1916), in the end a popular monarch. He built the **Ringstrasse** of beautiful buildings around the city, starting in 1857, and gradually developed a benevolent autocracy, and a modern industrialized economy.

The Danube was channelled, new bridges were constructed and in 1870 Vienna saw the first of its famous trams, or Strassenbahnen. **Schubert** was writing his lieder and, in *fin de siècle* Vienna, **Sigmund Freud** invented psychoanalysis. Coincidentally, Vienna acquired a reputation for the sort of unbridled café sensuality and eroticism that had characterized the Congress of Vienna at the start of the century.

### AMADEUS

Mozart lived in 20 different places in Vienna from October 1762 when he was six years old until his death on 5 December 1791.
**Jan–Dec 1768:**
Wipplingerstrasse 19 (aged 12).
**Jul–Sep 1773:** Tiefer Graben 18 (age 17).
He then settled permanently in Vienna and stayed at several other addresses.
**May–Sep 1781:**
Tuchlauben 6.
**Apr 1783 to Jan 1784:**
Judenplatz 3–4, where he composed his String Quartet in D Minor.
**Sep 1784 to Apr 1787:**
Domgasse 5.
**Jun 1788 to early 1789:**
Wahringer Strasse 26, where he composed Cosí fan tutte.
**Sep 1790 to 5 Dec 1791:**
Rauhensteingasse 8 (Magic Flute, Requiem).

## Invention and Innovation

Handsome **Karl Lueger**, Mayor, did much for Vienna, if not for his Jewish people, at the turn of the 19th century. He built gasworks, schools, old folks' homes, enlarged many of Vienna's parks and had the subway and tram systems electrified. Viennese journalist **Theodor Herzl** published *Der Judenstaat*, a work calling for and eventually leading to the creation of **Israel**. Artist **Gustav Klimt** and composer **Gustav Mahler** revolutionized the arts. The era saw the birth of Marxism, feminism, consumerism, Impressionism, cheap newspapers and popular leisure facilities, like the **Prater** Ferris wheel and funpark. **Albert Einstein** visited Vienna and stayed in Grinzing wine village.

## World War I

Rampant nationalism led to World War I. It was sparked by the assassination of **Archduke Franz Ferdinand**, heir to the Habsburg throne.

Millions died in the war, food was scarce, the empire was defeated, the coffee-house culture collapsed, and Vienna's first **socialist mayor** turned the postwar city into 'Red Vienna', with the construction of huge housing estates and major reforms in welfare, education and care for the workers. But this display of Marxist socialism created tension and led to the rise of the **Nazis**.

## Adolf Hitler

Although most Austrians wanted to link up with Germany at the end of World War I, by 1938 they sought their own independence. To pre-empt a referendum on the issue, Austrian-born Adolf Hitler marched into Austria and fabricated a plebiscite in favour of **Anschluss**, or unification, whereupon 42 synagogues were razed and the killings began. Some 250,000 Austrians were conscripted into the German World War II military, and nearly all died. It was worse for the Jewish community. Many had escaped, but 65,000 were slaughtered in the death camps. About

100,000 Austrians were imprisoned in Germany or in concentration camps, and 10,000 died in Gestapo custody. The Nazis in Austria did not have it all their own way, however, especially from 1944 onwards. **Resistance fighters**, code-named **05**, fought long and hard. About 2700 Jews were executed by the Nazis.

Vienna was bombed by the RAF and Allied forces on 52 occasions. The State Opera, Albertina Art Gallery, the Tiergarten in the Schönbrunn Palace gardens, all the city's bridges and 87,000 houses were hit; 24,000 Viennese lost their lives. Worse was the so-called 'liberation' of Vienna by the **Soviet army**. Encouraged by their officers, the troops raped some 90,000 Viennese women, and stole or removed practically everything in the city.

### The Third Man

The iconic 1949 film *The Third Man* with its portrayal of corrupt, bombed-out Vienna sums up the immediate postwar era. Like Berlin, Vienna was unfortunately within the Russian sector. And until the four victorious powers, which included the Americans and British, took joint control, the city suffered accordingly.

In 1955, to much jubilation, Austria got back its **independence**. Since then it has been a typical western parliamentary democracy and member of the European Union.

### GOVERNMENT AND ECONOMY

Half the population owns computers and every second person a car (Jaguars are popular). The average income is in excess of US$36,000 per annum, just below Japan. There was a 389% increase in value of trade from

**Below:** *Hitler addresses the people of Vienna in 1938, Heldenplatz, Hofburg.*

**OLD MAN RIVER**

The Danube's many tributaries used to create sprawling riverine meadows in the summer months and marshes stiff with ice in winter. And there have been an average of 10 destructive floods a year since time immemorial.

The Viennese have tried to control their tempestuous river since 1598, but it was not until 1870–75, using knowledge gained in the digging of the Suez Canal in Egypt, that serious rechannelling began. The Danube Canal was constructed, the Danube itself was straightened to allow for shipping and in 1972 a new channel (the New Danube) was cut, making four Danubes in all, although the Old Danube is more a series of recreational lakes. It is much bluer than the others because there is no current to stir up the riverbed limestone.

2000–2005. Austria's **exports** are valued at US$112 billion with a trade balance at US$3 billion. Its principal exports are machinery, motor vehicles, paper products, steel, textiles and foodstuffs, accounting for US$45 billion per annum. But it is in **high-tech services** (banking, finance, consulting, engineering) that it scores. Austria is one of the world's top 10 **tourist** destinations, earning the country US$15.6 billion.

Austrian **agriculture** only accounts for 2.2% of GDP: wine, potatoes, grains, dairy products, fruit, cattle and pigs. The country's natural resources include oil, coal, iron ore, copper, zinc, lignite and hydropower. About 85% of the country is rural and of that 17% is agricultural land.

The countryside, or *Länder*, usually votes conservative Catholic while Vienna is socialist. Austria flirted with Nazi fascism 70 years ago, which occasionally comes back to haunt it. Head of state is the directly elected Federal President, head of government the Chancellor. Every municipality has a powerful mayor. Parliament and Vienna's town hall, or Rathaus, are on the Ringstrasse. Austrian politics tend to swing left and right, making everyone uneasy. A former President and UN Secretary-General, **Kurt Waldheim**, took a hammering abroad if not in Austria on his war record, and one **Jörg Haider**, a former leader of the Austrian Freedom Party, occasionally rears his strident voice. The situation is exacerbated by Austria's (and the rest of Europe's) xenophobia about immigrants, which none of them can do without.

**Below:** *The red and white Austrian flag is often flown at the front of trams.*

## THE PEOPLE

There was a time in Vienna when you could not be received at the imperial court if you were 'not born'. Of the nobility, that is. Revolutions, wars and cheeky democracy put paid to that.

There are 8.1 million Austrians – roughly the number of Londoners – of whom 1.6 million live in Vienna. Some 15% are under 15 and 28% over 60. Adult literacy stands at 99% and women tend to have 1.4 babies

(so to speak). Some Viennese are **immigrants**, mainly from the former and neighbouring Soviet satellites and others from the Balkans and heavily populated Nigeria. Polite Pakistanis and Indians seem to monopolize the newspaper stands. The favourite names for girl babies, by far, are Leonie and Lena. And for boys, Tobias is the most popular, with Elias a losing second. About 58% of Vienna's tourists are from Germany.

**Above:** *The Volksgarten, one of Vienna's many green parks.*

Speak a few words from your German phrase book, and you will be greeted with a smile, a torrent of German and then fluent English, Vienna's second language.

## Smiles in Reserve

To an outsider, the Viennese can initially seem reserved. Head waiters in the grand cafés sometimes try their old-fashioned aloofness on newcomers. It's a historical act that goes with the sumptuous *bellestriste* décor and can quite easily be ameliorated with a smile.

Some interesting things about Viennese people: To be called 'Doktor' or 'Professor' in Vienna is apparently enormously comforting. Males in Austria are called up for national service. Men wear cashmere suits in the inner city; young women wear jeans and boots. Fast-food outlets, especially *wurst* (sausage) stands, are popular with commuters. Theatre, western classical music and opera are favourites. Above all, Vienna is a **pavement café society**.

Bicycle riding and walking are regular pastimes. There are bicycle paths fringing busy streets; pedestrians give way to cyclists. Transport is excellent, the tap water perfect, scientific research is on the increase, and there are some very noisy motorways along the Gürtel. Vienna is one of the safest cities in the world.

### SECRET DREAMS

Bellevue Höhe is a gentle, rather lonely grassy hill with a panoramic view of the city, not far from Grinzing. There are vineyards and behind them the great greenery of the Vienna Woods. There is a monument here to the inventor of psychoanalysis, Sigmund Freud (1856–1939), who discovered 'The Secret of Dreams'. He loved to stroll up here with his daughter Anna (who later became a child psychoanalyst), dressed in traditional Alpine walking gear and inevitably puffing away at one of his cigars.

## Language

The Viennese speak **German**. But it takes a German to distinguish the Viennese way of speaking. One tram ride watching the shops will throw up a host of English street advertising. The Viennese have many words and expressions all their own. They include some that are incomprehensible to other German speakers such as *Beisl*: tavern; *Stiftl*: wine glass; *Grüss Gott*: hello; *Hasse*: sausage.

The University of Vienna (there are no fewer than 13 universities in Vienna) offers inexpensive 9- to 12-week courses in German and there are several private institutions (e.g. Berlitz).

## Religion

In Vienna, **Judaism**, **Islam** and **Christianity** have always intermingled in war and peace, in repression and bigotry.

Today, half of Vienna's population is Catholic (750,000 at last count) with 660 churches. The city used to have a large Jewish population, but Nazi persecution devastated that. There are 46 mosques.

In Vienna, as in the Islamic world, the normal greeting is *Grüss Gott*, meaning 'God's greetings'. Most of Vienna's church interiors are Baroque and bewilderingly beautiful with their ceiling paintings, pillars of smoky marble, fancy gilt decoration, organs and trained choirs.

## Art

The **Kunsthistorisches Museum** shelters in magnificent array the world's fourth largest collection of paintings: Rubens' voluptuous nudes, Titian's glorious light and colour, Breughel's portrayal of simple folk in 'A country wedding' or 'Hunters in the snow.' Vienna has the world's largest Breughel collection. Then there is Rembrandt, Corregio, Caravaggio, Velázquez and Thomas Gainsborough, plus plenty of nature and wildlife paintings by Dürer. With 8000 paintings, the list is endless. There are some 80 museums and art galleries in Vienna, everything from a Madame-Tussaud-like

---

### TICKETS TO RIDE

Vienna has an interlinked transport system. A single daily ticket will get you on and off trams, buses, trains and metro for as long as you like. A weekly ticket, or *Wochenkarte*, costs €12.50. A monthly ticket, or *Monatskarte*, costs €45. You can get on and off and on again, 300 times if you like. Punch your ticket once in the on-board blue box and keep it on you. But everything operates on trust. The Vienna Card costs €18.50 and offers transport plus discounts in visitor attractions, shops and restaurants. Valid for 72 hours. A single-journey ticket costs €1.50. U-Bahn stations have multilingual vending machines, and *tabak* (tobacconists) also sell tickets.

Criminals' museum to the private Third Man film museum. Local Viennese artists over the last 150 years have included such Art Nouveau (Jugendstil) masters as Gustav Klimt and Egon Schiele. A whole new **Museums Quartier** was built in 2001, one of the 10 largest cultural complexes in the world, offering exhibitions, music, the MUMOK Museum of modern art, the Leopold Museum with some 5000 paintings of Austrian art, even a children's paddling pool. You can learn to dance here, have a meal, gaze at 2500 exhibits in the Tobacco Museum, visit Math Space or treat the young to the ZOOM activity museum. Some three million people visit the Museums Quartier Wien each year.

## Architecture

Vienna is a city of Baroque palaces and Gothic churches. Conscious of this historic heritage, and with one or two forgettable exceptions, the only high-rise buildings in Vienna are across the Danube, out of town. These are the modern neo-brutalist skyscrapers of the Vienna International Centre and UNO City. Surrounded by the gunmetal high-rises of Donau City, this 1979 scrum of scalloped steel and glass huddles in moody isolation. Inside, behind tight security, an army of Unocrats of the International Atomic Energy Agency, the Commission for Infectious diseases, the High Commission for Refugees (UNHCR) and the Industrial Organization UNIDO, beaver away at their computers, saving the world.

New buildings have always been greeted with great suspicion by Viennese coffee-sippers, and are only reluctantly accepted once they have dissected every aspect of their construction.

### ROCK OF AGES

No wonder Harry Lime, *The Third Man*, went for the sewers to escape. There are 182km (113 miles) of storm sewer systems, in which a man can stand, deep down beneath Vienna's busy streets. Some buildings have five levels of cellars, many unintentionally connected, others brick-walled monastic cellars that were used to keep wine cool. Some, today, are restaurants. These cellars were used as bomb shelters in World War II.

The Inner City sits on top of an ancient compound of earth and debris 9m (29ft) thick, some of it going back to Roman times. There has not been much building in the old city, but whenever there is, it inevitably brings discoveries. An old medieval chapel was unearthed in Stephansplatz when the U-Bahn was being constructed.

**Below:** *MUMOK Museum specializes in way out art.*

## PEOPLE OF THE BOOK

Many Jews were forced out of their homeland in Palestine 1900 years ago. Their diaspora took some to Vienna in the 12th century. They soon came up against Christian bigotry. Accused of being 'Christ's killers', they were bullied, tortured, robbed and murdered. The Jews were twice expelled from Vienna, in 1420 and 1670. Restrictions on Jews were only lifted after the 1848 Revolution. By 1910, 10% (180,000) of Vienna's population was Jewish. Hitler's 1938 Anschluss led to 65,000 Jews being murdered in the Holocaust.

Famous Jewish Viennese have included Sigmund Freud, composers Gustav Mahler, Arnold Schönberg and Johann Strauss, and writer Arthur Schnitzler. Nine-tenths of Viennese culture in the 19th century was promoted, nurtured or in some cases even created by Jews.

Modern buildings in Vienna include those of the new **Museums Quartier**, **Haas Haus**' blue glass building opposite the Cathedral, the fabulously colourful **Hundertwasser House** and the innovative crooked-style **Gasometer** makeover.

Most suburban streets in Vienna are lined with endless four- to five-storey blocks, some attractively decorated, others grey faceless cement, quickly built after the war by unions and socialist groups to house the poor. Each has a date and who built it in proud letters. The severity of the blocks is only broken by the lively shops at ground level, the flower beds at corners, and phalanxes of lime and chestnut trees.

### Film and TV

There are two state TV stations, neither famous for enlightened creativity.

Vienna's excellent International Film Festival, the **Viennale**, takes place in October. Most films shown in Vienna are in German but check in the newspapers *Der Standard* or *Die Presse* for listings in English. 'OF' means it's in the original and 'OmeU' means it has English subtitles. Arts International in the Innere Stadt shows English films, as does the English Cinema. The

**Right:** *All of Vienna haggled over the construction of the modern Haas Haus, Stephansplatz.*

Bellaria specializes in old black-and-white Austrian-German movies, while the Burg Kino regularly features *The Third Man* in its original English. There is cinema under the stars in the Augarten from July to August.

*Bride of the Wind*, a film on Gustav Mahler's wife, Alma, is intriguing. *The Piano Teacher*, based on Elfriede Jelinek's novel, won three prizes at Cannes.

**Above:** *Sorrow and symphony are reflected in the eyes of this Viennese street violinist.*

## Music and Opera

Vienna is probably the most musical city in the world. Much of western classical music was developed here: Mozart, Schubert, Bruckner, Schönberg, Beethoven, Brahms – the list is endless. The **Vienna Philharmonic Orchestra** is possibly the world's best with the **Vienna Symphony** not far behind. The **Vienna State Opera** and the **Musikverein** are magnets to all visitors, as is the **Vienna Boys' Choir** who have performed in the same Royal Chapel for 500 years. In Vienna you can see collections of ancient Stradivarius violins and visit the graves of famous composers.

There are at least 30 musical venues and dozens of churches offering music, with Gregorian chant a speciality. There are 50 rock 'n' pop gigs weekly, plenty of jazz and café concerts. In effect, music in Vienna is round every corner even if it is only a street busker on his Strassenmusik cello. There are 16 theatres in Vienna with the **Volksoper**, **Burgtheater** and **Volkstheater** probably the most popular and the **English Theatre** offering regular performances.

## Literature

Two hundred years ago, Vienna was the cultural capital of the German-speaking world. **Austrian fiction** includes the works of Josef Roth (*Radetzky March*),

### OH, THOSE ROMANS

Adolf Hitler, struggling to sketch the spring tulips outside the Sperl Coffee House 100 years ago, may have yearned for a 1000-year Reich. But the only ones to pull it off, before or since, were the ancient Romans. Their brutal empire collapsed around AD500. Ironically they often preferred to speak Greek, but they left us an incredible legacy of law, language, literature and construction, in some ways the heart of European culture, plus a few hidden ruins to delight Viennese archaeologists: a Bath House, a terracotta drain, walls below Maria am Gestade church and paving slabs. The Stephansdom has an inscribed Roman gravestone in one of its arches. The best ruins are below Hoher Markt, where two Roman houses complete with underfloor heating were excavated.

playwright Arthur Schnitzler (his *Dream Story* was the inspiration for Stanley Kubrick's film, *Eyes Wide Shut)*, Stefan Zweig (*The Burning Secret*), Robert Musil (*The Man without Qualities*) and Thomas Bernhard's cutting critique of postwar Austria, *Wittgenstein's Nephew*.

Writers such as Elfriede Jelinek, Peter Handke (still among the world's top writers) and Thomas Bernard, all born between 1931 and 1946, slammed Austria and Vienna's interpretation of its postwar self as a victim of the Nazis, Soviets and world opinion. To them, Austria was a nation of criminals with a criminal past, for which society dubbed them *Nestbeschmutzer*, or nest foulers. **Elfriede Jelinek** was awarded the **2004 Nobel Prize** for literature.

## Coffee to go, Coffee to stay

For many, café culture is the most delightful aspect of the Viennese laid-back lifestyle.

The word coffee comes to us via Italian, Turkish and ultimately the Arabic word *qahwah* (*see* panel, this page), which strangely also means wine.

In Vienna there is a saying that guests at cafés are emigrants, exiles escaping from everyday life in the cosy atmosphere where writers, musicians and artists argue politics, religion and philosophy. You don't have to be literary. Just sit, keep drinking and read the many multi-language newspapers for free.

In the grand old cafés, you can order coffee prepared in some 20 different ways. Coffee upside-down, or *Kaffee Verkehrt*, is hot foamed milk with espresso served in a glass, the *Verlängerter* is a stretched espresso with cream and Cointreau. Then we get into the cakes and meal menus, and lengthy lists of steady-your-nerves-before-commuting-home wines, beers and spirits. Go into **Café Central** in the inner city, wait until you are allocated a table (smoking or non), hand your coat over for hanging up, select a paper, order your favourite and people-watch for an hour or two while the pianist or violinist plays a little Schubert. True Viennese style.

**Opposite:** *Sachertorte, the quintessential and world-famous Viennese chocolate cake.*

The best grand cafés include **Sperl** (the 19th-century décor remains unchanged), **Landtmann**, **Hawelka** and **Weimar**. If needs must, you can also buy an inexpensive coffee-to-go at underground stations.

## What to Eat

**Wiener Schnitzel** when it comes in very thin *schnitzel*, or slices, of veal is scrumptious, a bit filling otherwise. The **strudels** are always superb, as are the exotic **cakes**. Each big café seems to have its own *torte*, or cake, to compete with the ubiquitous layered *chocolate Sachertorte* of the café of the same name. The Viennese choose from some 20 different **breads** and **rolls** at breakfast, or *Frühstück* (it means 'early bit'). You can't go wrong with rye. **Cheeses** include the hard black-cased *Weinkäse*, the soft *Liptauer* spread served at Heuriger wine taverns near the Vienna Woods, and the *Kracher* with its intense aroma and ivory and emerald-green marbling.

Vienna likes its **meat**: pork and beef. The dishes are inevitably excellent but delicate they are not, except in the top restaurants like the Kinsky. Boar à la Asterix is a speciality during the hunting season. **Soups** are always tasty. Try the *Hühnersuppe* (chicken with noodles).

The nomenclature of dishes is often different from that in Germany. A menu is called a *Speisekarte*. A basket of rolls with your meal is always extra, but you'll only be charged for those you actually eat. A sausage, roll and mustard from a *wurst* street stand is a must.

> ### TURKISH DELIGHT
>
> The Turkish crescent moon emblem gave it its shape and the French may have developed it into every Parisian's nibble, but it was the Viennese who invented the lovely pastry we call croissant, or in Vienna-speak *Beugel* or *Kipferl*. The French adopted it when Empress Maria Theresia's daughter Marie Antoinette (who probably never said 'let the people eat cake') married the King of France and lost her head in the Revolution. Grünangergasse 8 in the old city is supposed to have baked the place where the first croissant was baked in 1683. Look out for Vienna's historic bakeries. Their names and bakery wares are usually written in gold on black glass tablets.

There are dozens of Chinese and Japanese restaurants, usually with fancy dragon doors and 'Running Sushi' or 'Sushi Wong' names. Staff in Viennese restaurants all have black leather wallets slung from their belts like sixguns and they will often scribble your bill out in front of you on a pad, asking you what you ordered. Quite a few restaurants have *grande dame* lady owners.

Irish pubs offer 'Great Australian Bite Burgers' and other delicacies, and you'll find kebab stands at every tram intersection – Persian, Indian, African, Italian, even one called Good Morning Vietnam. By the way, always ask for *Schwarz* (black) tea, or you'll get lemon.

### QUEEN OF TARTS

The best cafés bake their own *torten*. Most are death by whipped cream.
*Apfelstrudel*: you have not lived until you've had Viennese Apfelstrudel.
*Easterházy*: layers of sponge and cream, white icing and a feather motif.
*Sachertorte*: chocolate sponge cake coated in dark chocolate with a fine layer of apricot jam underneath.
*Guglhupf*: marble cake baked in a fluted ring and sliced – Sigmund Freud's choice.
*Topfen-Joghurt, Linzertorte*: sponge cake, strawberries, yoghurt and cream shaped like a railway tunnel.

### What to Drink

Most **wine** grown on the slopes around Vienna is Grüner Veltliner, a young white wine with a fruity bouquet, the drier the better. Then there are Rieslings from the Wachau on the Danube River hills. The red wines, the experts will tell you, have improved dramatically in recent years. Try Blaufränkisch (Blue Frank), but not the inexpensive supermarket variety. A definite is *Most*, the juice of freshly pressed grapes prior to fermentation into wine. Or even better, *Sturm*, sold in open bottles and only available in autumn – a sort of halfway house wine. The cloudy unfiltered young *Staubiger* (dusty one) and the 'This Year's', or *Heuriger,* are excellent. In restaurants you often buy wine by the glass, which is equal to an eighth or quarter of a litre. A bottle of wine contains seven-eighths of a litre.

Austria is the world's fifth-largest consumer of **beer** per person. Half a pint is a *Seidl* and half a litre is a *Krügerl*. There are rare land beers from the country, *Schankbier*, or draught 12.5% *Vollbier*. Careful. And then there's the harder-hitting, amber-coloured Bock beer. *Double Bock* is strictly for mountaineers and miners. The most popular Viennese canned beer is *Ottakringer* or, in patois, *Blech* (cans from the brewery's 16th district).

## FOOD FOR THE VOLK

In medieval times, on market day, a flag would be raised. Until noon the only people allowed to purchase from the various markets were courtiers, clergy and citizens. Everyone else had to wait. The streets around Stephansdom reflect the food-oriented priorities of the populace at a time when famine was not uncommon. There is the Fleischmarkt (Meat Market), Kohlmarkt (Cabbage Market) where today designer brands are sold, Bauermarkt (Farmers' Market) and Getreidemarkt (Grain Market).

**Opposite:** *Viennese, like Parisians, only buy that morning's freshest breads.* **Left:** *Landbier is a special boutique beer brewed in the countryside.*

# 2. Ancient City: Stephansdom

No matter which exit escalator you take, you will see the lacy twin spires of the sandstone **Votivkirche** (Votive church) when you emerge from Schottentor Underground. It was built 130 years ago to launch Kaiser Franz Josef's demolition of the old city walls and the building of a Ringstrasse of grand buildings surrounding his palace. And to praise the Lord for his narrow escape from an assassination attempt that one János Libényi, a Hungarian nationalist and tailor by trade, made on him in the winter of 1853 in the cobbled alleyways of nearby Mölker Bastei. It is said only a button on his stiff collar saved him from the dagger thrust.

## Ancient Walls ★★★

Directly opposite the new university, round the corner from Schottentor, is a massive plinth capped by a gold-winged angel. Behind and to the left of this monument, a ramp leads up to part of the old city's medieval star-shaped **Mölker Bastei** ramparts and Pasqualatihaus where Ludwig van Beethoven, the illustrious German composer, lived for part of his 35 years in Vienna.

## Dreimäderlhaus

Next door at No. 10 is the 'Three maidens' or **Dreimäderlhaus**. Whether the honour of the three ladies here (all sisters) survived the romantic attentions of Viennese Franz Schubert is a matter for conjecture. He was a bit of a lad and died penniless at 31, of syphilis, a killer pre-penicillin. However, the house is

### DON'T MISS

**★★★ Stephansdom:** Gothic cathedral.
**★★★ Schottenstift:** monastic produce shop.
**★★★ Holocaust Memorial:** 65,000 murdered.
**★★ Mölker Bastei:** old city walls.
**★★ Freyung Market:** organic foods.
**★★ St Ruprechts:** the oldest church in Vienna.

**Opposite:** *Neo-Gothic statues on the outside wall of the Votivkirche.*

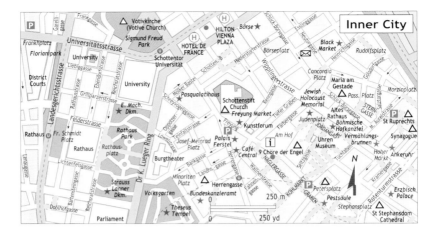

**Opposite:** *Palais Ferstel,
built by Heinrich Ferstel
between 1856 and 1860.*

not named after the ladies, but after a 1920s opera. In
front of a paint-peeling doorway is a sign, No. 8,
Mölker Bastei. This is the exact spot where Orson
Welles (who played Harry Lime) was filmed, back in
the iconic 1949 movie ***The Third Man*** with its haunting
zither music.

### Schottenstift ★★★

Schottenstift monastery, dating back 850 years, was
named after Scottish (but actually Irish) monks. Only a
few corners remain of its ancient Romanesque interior,
now 18th-century Baroque – lush marble columns,
gold flourishes, pastel ceiling paintings and doleful
pictures of heaven-hallucinating saints. The highlight
in the museum is a multipanelled hinged **altarpiece**,
featuring Joseph and Mary's biblical flight with the
baby Jesus from King Herod to safety in Egypt 2000
years ago. Rather charmingly, medieval Vienna forms
the backdrop.

### The Freyung ★★

The name of the 'Freyung' facing the monastery
church and museum means sanctuary. In an age of
banditry and uncertainty, monasteries were often forti-

fied refuges around which farming and villages developed. It is an oblong, cobbled square flanked by the 1946 nymph-decorated Austria fountain. Freyung hums with action. There are two **pavement cafés** with snappy service, one specializing in exotic ice-cream sundaes. The ad hoc **stalls** in the **market** sell organic products (the largest selection in Austria, they say), toys, baskets, home-made jams, jewellery, fruit schnapps (corn schnapps is more a German speciality), with parties of ladies enjoying a glass of wine at the collapsible tables.

Freyung, in the days before football fever and pop concerts, was quite the entertainment centre as it was here that public executions were held. Here, too, is the **Schubladenkastenhaus**, or Chest of Drawers house, built in 1774. The **Café Central** is round the corner. It has vaulted ceilings, smart-jacketed waiters, newspapers from all over the world and elegant coffees, and was the intelligentsia's favourite 100 years ago.

### Am Hof

High above the corner of the street that leads to Am Hof, the largest enclosed square in Vienna, is a **statuette** of a Turkish warrior, scimitar in hand. Fighting the Turks centuries ago was always more exciting and spiritually rewarding than scuffling with Swedish protestants and hungry Hungarians. Watch out for the *fiaker* hackney cabs (about €40 for a half-hour group ride). The drivers have long coats, whips and bowler hats; some are women.

---

**THE LOCAL GROCER**

As at Fortnum and Mason in London, Meinl am Graben in Vienna is where you can purchase anything a connoisseur of the good life could wish: jams by Staud, wines by Kracher, chocolates by Zotter, cheeses, fish, pastries. There is a wine and sushi bar upstairs to cater to your hedonism. And if you're feeling just a touch guilty, some of the products are Fair Trade so you can take comfort in the thought that you are helping someone in a hot faraway land.

## VIENNA'S PALACES

At the height of its 640-year geographical and military power, the Austrian Empire ruled over 50 million people with Vienna as its capital. Naturally, everyone who wanted to be someone came to Vienna to be noticed, and to build a palais – a schloss away from the schloss, so to speak. The palaces that surround the Hofburg include Palais Ferstel, built in 1860 and home of the Café Central. Palais Harrach is much older, rebuilt in 1690 after the Turks destroyed it. The Kinsky Palais was built in 1713–16 by renowned architect Johann von Hildebrandt for the Daun family.

**Below:** *Antiques market, Am Hof.*

Am Hof quite often transforms itself into a **market** with antiques, food stalls, books, accordion buskers and benches on which to sit and admire the historic buildings enclosing the square. Am Hof means at the Royal Court. The medieval Babenberger tribe built their palace here, as did the Habsburgs who replaced them. In the humble **Collalto Palace**, child genius Mozart stunned Vienna in 1762 with his first performance at the age of six.

### Judenplatz ★★★
A quiet lane leads from Am Hof to a cobbled square surrounded by gracious buildings. In the middle of this square stands a silent stone block the height of two men. The **Judenplatz Jewish Holocaust Memorial** was designed by British sculptor, Rachel Whiteread. It has no colour, no ornamentation, just two closed doors, a raised plinth and row after row of chiselled books, each frozen page commemorating the loss of the 65,000 Austrian men, women and children slaughtered by Hitler's Nazis in the Holocaust, simply because they were Jews. Anti-Semitism is Europe's oldest disease. As a result of the

**Left:** *Judenplatz Holocaust Memorial. Each stone, a book, a life lost.*

destruction of several gospels that gave the Jews a sympathetic hearing in the early Christian church, the myth developed among Christians in Europe that somehow it was the Jewish people rather than a corrupt power-hungry hierarchy who murdered Jesus. Thus anti-Semitism was born.

A relief, *Zum Grossen Jordan* (To the Great Jordan), on one wall of the **oldest house on the square** celebrates a typical pogrom with the words: *thus the flame rising furiously through the whole city, in 1421, purged the terrible crimes of 'the Hebrew dogs'.* Two hundred Jews were burned at the stake on this occasion.

In 1896, Viennese journalist **Theodor Herzl** was the first to call for a Jewish state in his *Der Judenstaat*, which eventually led to the creation of modern Israel.

### Altes Rathaus

The **Old Rathaus** has no doubt seen a few rodent councillors in its time, but it actually means Town Hall. Its delicate ironwork portico leads inside to the Archives of the Austrian anti-Nazi Resistance.

### Maria am Gestade

To the left of the Rathaus in the cobbled Salvatorgasse is **Maria am Gestade**, Mary of the Riverbank, a fine

**Above:** *Rathaus by night.*
**Opposite:** *Ankeruhr's puppet clock goes into action on each hour.*

---

---

church preserved in the ancient 14th-century Gothic style. Its tower is 56m (180ft) high. Being near the river, it was a favourite with Danube fishing folk; today, Czech worshippers attend this church.

### St Ruprechts Church ★★

The oldest church in Vienna is **St Ruprechts**, reached by a flight of steps above busy Schwedenplatz and the Danube. Ruprecht was chosen by the Danube boatmen, salt merchants, to be their patron saint. Salt was extremely valuable in medieval times. The small and squat Romanesque ivy-covered church lies on the foundation of an 8th-century church, rebuilt and altered many times.

### Bermuda Triangle

Back from St Ruprechts church, little cobbled alleys (an area in the 1980s so packed with bars and lost revellers that it was nicknamed the Bermuda Triangle) with small restaurants and elegant high cupolas lead to the only **Jewish Synagogue** to escape the destruction of the 1938 Nazi Kristallnacht. Ironically throughout World War II, the **Austrian Resistance**, 05, had its headquarters in this area at Ruprechtsplatz 5, a stone's throw from the Hotel Metropol's Gestapo torture centre.

Cross the frantic Rotenturmstrasse that leads down to the Danube Canal and Marienbrücke and you will come to two **Greek Orthodox churches** and the 500-year-old **Griechenbeisl**, literally Greek pub. Its seven small rooms have seen the likes of Tarzan (Johnny Weismüller), Schubert, Liebe Augustin (or darling Augustin, a popular Vienna busker of the 17th century), Bismarck the German statesman, Mozart, Johnny Cash (Walk the Line), Mark Twain and Graf Zeppelin.

## Hoher Markt Square

You need a good imagination standing in Hoher Markt Square to realize that this, the Roman Forum, the oldest square and fish market in Vienna, was (nearly 2000 years ago) the centre of Roman Vienna or Vindobona. Drab 50-year-old buildings surround the busy square with its centrepiece attraction, the **Marriage Fountain**, or Vermählungsbrunnen, designed by 17th-century Viennese architect Fischer von Erlach.

There is a café here called, naturally, 'The Limes' after the Roman defensive line built to keep the always infiltrating German tribes at bay. In its urban-chic design it is light years away from a rough Roman camp, but its mélange coffee in delicate white cups would have braced the sword arm of any legionary.

Today's main attraction in the Square is the **Ankeruhr**, or clock bridge, spanning two buildings of the Anker insurance company. Designed in 1914, it is a heavily gilded mechanical clock across whose face, on the hour, jerk-glides one of twelve characters from Vienna's colourful history.

## Stephansdom ★★★

There are 660 Catholic churches in Vienna. Head, shoulders, surrounding platz and soaring spire above the many Catholic churches in Vienna is the great Stephansdom (**St Stephen's Cathedral**), with its 137m (450ft) Steffl, or steeple, which visitors in good wind can reach by climbing up the stairway. The cornerstone of today's

**Below:** *The intricately
patterned multicoloured
tiles of Stephansdom.*

church was laid in 1137, although much of the cathedral was built in the 14th century to its present Gothic
style. Its interior was given a Baroque makeover during
the 17th century. In 1711, the 'Pummerin,' an immense
bell, was cast from captured Turkish cannons and
placed in the North, or pagan, tower. (The church has
four towers.) By 1732 the bells called the faithful to an
average of 150 masses celebrated in the cathedral per day.

The cathedral saw the Turkish wars, hand-to-hand
fighting in the 1809 Napoleonic conflict, and half of it
was destroyed by fire following Russian artillery attacks
that hit surrounding houses in 1945.

### Roof of Many Colours

The roof of St Stephen's Cathedral is 110m (361ft) long
and is pitched in such a way that the rain's drain-off
power cleans it. It consists of 605 tons of steel – replacing a veritable forest of 3000 Gothic tree trunks – and
230,000 glazed and zigzag roof tiles, each of which
weighs 2.5kg (5.5lb).

**Left:** *One of St Stephen's Cathedral's many altars.*

## LONG-RANGE BOMBERS

Until 1944 Vienna was out of range of British long-range bombers. Everything changed the following year when there were 52 raids. All hit non-military targets. They included, on 12 March 1945, the Vienna State Opera which caught fire, destroying all the decorations and costumes. In mid-March 1945 Schönbrunn's historic zoo, the oldest in the world, was hit, killing two-thirds of the animals. On 12 April 1945 the already damaged St Stephen's Cathedral was hit. Some 8769 people were killed in the raids, all bridges destroyed and only 41 civilian vehicles survived. You can still come across bomb craters in the Vienna Woods.

## Vision of Beauty

When the sun pours through Stephansdom's vast array of needle windows, the dappled light fragments the interior into a treasure chest. It lights up the patterned

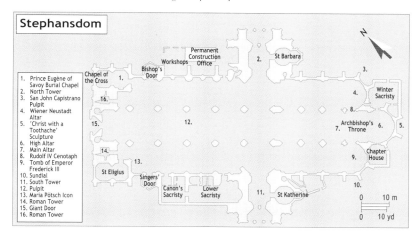

Stephansdom

1. Prince Eugène of Savoy Burial Chapel
2. North Tower
3. San John Capistrano Pulpit
4. Wiener Neustadt Altar
5. 'Christ with a Toothache' Sculpture
6. High Altar
7. Main Altar
8. Rudolf IV Cenotaph
9. Tomb of Emperor Frederick III
10. Sundial
11. South Tower
12. Pulpit
13. Maria Pötsch Icon
14. Roman Tower
15. Giant Door
16. Roman Tower

floor of the central nave, the huge fluted columns, each filigree pillar decorated by a life-size saint (107 of them), dozens of painting-backed altars, stained glass, unbelievably soaring vaulting, gilt, and carvings of the Madonna including the 1320 one called *Madonna of the Domestics*, where early-to-work servant girls heard mass. As composer Frédéric Chopin wrote (Christmas 1830): 'it is an immense space in which silence reigns'.

### The Toothache Lord

On one interior wall of the North tower, which was never finished and subsequently topped with a Baroque cupola, there is a **statue of Jesus** called the 'Christ with a Toothache.' It was at one time mounted on the outside of the church and drunken night-time passers-by would mock Jesus' agonized face, asking if he had a toothache, whereupon they were all afflicted by toothache themselves and only cured when they begged forgiveness of the statue.

The working draft plans of the cathedral, the world's largest Gothic collection, are kept in Vienna's **Historical Museum** in Karlsplatz.

**Opposite:** *Pavement restaurants seat hundreds either side of the Black Death Monument in Graben.*
**Right:** *Young men dressed as 18th-century courtiers encourage visitors to attend concert performances.*

## Stephansplatz

As in the old medieval city, all roads (mud tracks at the time) lead, star-like, to the **cathedral** and its busy and huge cobbled **square**. There are nearby food stands, hackney cabs by the north wall, hawkers of Mozart concerts in 18th-century costume, leaflet distributors, ice-cream vendors, flower sellers, tour groups, genuine pilgrims and a rolling half-an-hour-each repertory of musicians, dancers and buskers entertaining the ever-moving crowds.

## Graben

In 1918 it was the great influenza epidemic that killed millions. In medieval Europe it was bubonic plague, the **Black Death**.

Carried by rats and rat fleas in an era when people lived close-packed, often in hovels, and had little idea of sanitation or medicine, the effect was calamitous. Death often came within days. In Vienna during one scourge, 500 died daily.

Graben, near the cathedral, is a pedestrian mall of restaurants and gold card shoppers. Other than its eclectic Victorian underground loos, its centrepiece is the 1692 **Black Death Monument** (Pestsäule or Plague Pillar), a work of convoluted art commemorating the city's deliverance from the 1679 plague. Cherubs and saints piggy-back one on the other in a cloud of detailed sculpture and ethereal imagination, all covered in netting to deter pigeons with inelegant digestive habits.

### OPERA FOR THE PEOPLE

The hills of Vienna may no longer be alive with the Sound of Music, but the Volksoper certainly hasn't noticed. It is a regular feature in the giant cream building in Währingerstrasse, as in Johan Strauss's 'Die Fledermaus' and Queen's 'We will rock you'. The Volksoper features 100 performances a year. The audience often joins in.

# 3. Ancient City: Hofburg

The Hofburg was the Imperial Palace from where the **Habsburgs** ruled Austria for 640 years going back to Rudolf of Habsburg (from *Habichtsberg*, or Hawk mountain), a minor German warrior prince in Swabia. It was he who gave the Duchy of Vienna to his son, Albrecht.

Over the centuries, the Hofburg became a city within the Inner City, a vast complex of buildings, gardens, squares and churches all linked in a haphazard yet solid demonstration of power. Stand in the Volksgarten and look across lawns and carriageways to the semi-circular Neue Burg, or New Castle, and one cannot fail to be impressed by the size, sumptuousness and yes, vanity, of the dynasty.

**Heldenplatz**, or Heroes' Square, is where Hitler, who was always one for a melodramatic setting, announced the *Anschluss*, or Union of Austria, to Germany in 1938. Today, the vast two-thousand-room interior has been replaced by a multifloored complex of **galleries and museums**: Ethnology Museum, Ancient Musical Instruments, Papyrus Museum, Arms and Armour collection, and the Ephesus Museum with antiques pinched from the ancient trading city of Ephesus, now in Turkey. (St Paul wrote a long epistle to the Ephesians telling them about it 1900 years ago.) Don't miss the 40m (131ft) long Roman Parthian battle frieze.

## Hofburg's Museums

In the **Collection of Ancient Musical Instruments** in the Hofburg are some marked with a green dot. That means

## DON'T MISS

**\*\*\* St Michael's Gate**: domes and gilt and classical statues mark the huge entrance to the Imperial Palace.
**\*\*\* Spanish Riding School**: fabulously trained Lipizzaner horses perform balletic jumps.
**\*\*\* Royal Treasury**: among dazzling displays, the world's largest cut emerald.
**\*\*\* Royal Apartments**: the Habsburgs ruled for 640 years.
**\*\* Albertina**: 1.5 million works of graphic art.

**Opposite:** *St Michael's Gate, the vast entrance to the Hofburg Palace.*

**Opposite:** *Neue Burg and the Volksgarten's lovely lawns.*

you can play them. The Renaissance instrument collection is the best in the world. One claviorgan even replicates a birdsong. Archduke Ferdinand of Savoy collected many of these, some, miniatures, made for his children. He liked playing on the ivory-bottomed pear-shaped lute, a sort of troubadour's guitar, which he plucked and sang of love and derring-do. There is a tortoiseshell violin, a glass harmonica, a crystal flute and a piano with six rows of keys once played by Beethoven.

The collection of Arms and Armour is strictly for the boys. There is jousting tackle and suits of armour going back to 1460 – lots of knights were injured until armour improved. Turkish weaponry from the two great sieges of Vienna is well displayed. In the Palace Gardens behind the Neue Burg and Palm House there is a variety of monuments to miscellaneous emperors and one of Mozart.

The **Museum of Ethnology** boasts an exotic potpourri of African, Oriental, Polynesian, Chinese, Eskimo and South American exhibits. A colourful Aztec feather head-dress was for many years believed to have belonged to Aztec Emperor Moctezuma and given as a gift to Conquistador Hernándo Cortés 500 years ago.

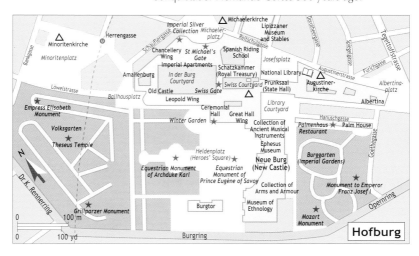

## Royal Apartments ★★★

The Hofburg, a UNESCO Heritage Site, voluptuously spreads itself over 18 wings and 19 courtyards, as each sovereign over 600 years added and changed the buildings. To the north of Heldenplatz is the **Great Hall Wing**, the **Winter Garden** – which is a building more than a garden – and the **Ceremonial Hall**. In front the *fiakers* trot on by and visitors pause to take a picture and sip from water bottles, overawed by all the grandeur. The Old Castle's **Leopold Wing** has over 200 symmetrical windows. It faces onto *In der Burg*, the Old Castle courtyard. The huge azure and gold bell-like cupola above **St Michael's Gate** is straight ahead. The official entrance to the Hofburg is a semi-circular wing with three huge copper-blue domes and impressive mythological statuary. The **Imperial Apartments** occupy one end: dressing room, grand salon, Empress Elisabeth's rooms, drawing room. Kaiserin Sisi was said to be capable of spending all morning getting bathed and dressed. The other half of this building is the **Chancellery Wing** where the Kaiser received courtiers in classic bow-and-approach style.

### BURY THEM DEEP

The crypt below St Michael's church in Kohlmarkt dates back 800 years to medieval times. But the rows of wooden coffins, some decorated with angels, skulls and hour glasses, are only 400 years old. The constant coolness of the temperature has preserved the corpses, hair, clothes, skin, boots, rosaries and burial sheets. Some coffins have collapsed, others, rather grander, still have their iron carry-rings. By the time the practice of burying beneath churches was abandoned in 1783, 4000 well-to-do folk had been left to wither away in spiritual seclusion. The floor level has risen over the centuries, the ground being made up of crushed bones.

## PILGRIMS' PROGRESS

When April arrives it is time for Christian women and men to go on pilgrimage. The 14th-century English poet Geoffrey Chaucer would probably not have recognized today's Danube pilgrims. But the practice is no different: walking, praying, staying overnight at an inn. The Jacobsweg route along the Danube northwest of Vienna, through forest and hills and clearly signposted, covers a distance of 800km (497 miles). Some walk alone, some go by bicycle. Some even hitch a ride in a Danube leisure boat. There's a book mapping the route: *Auf dem Jacobsweg durch Österreich* by Peter Lindenthal.

## Nuptial Despair

Kaiser Franz Josef's **bedroom** was a simple single iron bed affair. He and his wife Elisabeth were estranged almost from the day they were married. She produced the requisite male heir and then spent most of her life travelling around Europe.

The rooms before the Kaiser's apartments have recently been turned into a six-roomed **Sisi Museum**. Sisi is something of a Viennese cult, cleverly sustained by Vienna's tourism gurus. Franz Xavier Winterhalter's portrait of her in a star-spangled gown and flowing locks is everywhere. You can sample her sad little poems framed on the walls, excerpts from films made on her life and see the many statues of the Imperial couple. Here, too, is her weighing machine (she was very 21st century in her weight watching), her fabulous jewellery and a reconstruction of her personal railway carriage saloon. The denouement is a sepulchral apparition of her which, to the cries of mournful seagulls, quavers the line from her poem: '*Eine Möwe bin*

**Right:** *Interior view of the magnificent cupola of St Michael's Gate.*

*ich, von keinen land'* (a seagull am I with no land to call my own). She was a very unhappy woman, her life a classic of forced marriage and subsequent despair. Starkly lit is the sharpened file with which she was stabbed to death. Her assassination ensured that the myth of married bliss, honed to perfection by Romy Schneider's performance in the 1950s film *Forever My Love*, lived on in the bitter-sweet melancholy of all Viennese coffee-drinkers. No-one does death better than the Viennese.

## Royal Treasury ★★★

The gilded writing above the claret and grey-striped portal of the **Swiss Gate** in the Old Palace, erected in 1552, lists Ferdinand's many imperial territories. It ends with the letters, 'ZC' or 'etc'. Past the steps to the **Burgkapelle**, the chapel where the Vienna Boys' Choir sings on Sundays, is the Schatzkammer, or **Royal Treasury**. Here can be found not only the Crown Jewels but a treasure trove of secular and ecclesiastical artefacts, many crafted in medieval times: coronation robes, Habsburg ruling insignia, symbols of honour and dazzling jewellery. There is an agate bowl at one time thought to be the Holy Grail used by Jesus at the Last Supper, the quest of many chivalrous knights.

The world's largest cut emerald, a whopping 2680-carat Colombian wonder, is on display. In the **Sacred Treasury** there are pieces of first disciple Veronica's veil, with which she wiped the blood off Jesus' face. Religious relic veneration has a long tradition in European Catholicism. Here they include the Holy Lance which pierced Christ's side on the cross (unfortunately dated to the 8th century), a strip of Baby Jesus' bib, a piece of the Last Supper tablecloth and a tooth from John the Baptist.

The Crown Jewels of the Holy Roman Empire were taken to Nürnberg, their traditional home, in 1938 by Hitler but returned to Vienna by the Americans in 1945. The Holy Roman Empire crown is believed to have been used at the coronation of Charlemagne in

---

### VIENNESE LANGUAGE

As in all cities, Vienna has slang and a dialect all of its own. *Es ist wurst* (it is sausage), for example, means 'not important'. *Marie* means 'money' and telling the time can be different:
5.15: *Viertel Sechs*
5.30: *Halb Sechs*
5.45: *Dreiviertel Sechs*
*Mahlzeit!* (literally meaning 'lunchtime') is a greeting you would use around noon, instead of 'good morning' or 'good afternoon'. *Na* is 'No' and *Habe die Ehre*, meaning 'have the honour' is said instead of saying goodbye. To a visitor the strangest of all is *Nehyore*, roughly translated as 'more or less', 'well' or 'sort of'.

800, but in fact was fashioned 100 years later. Charlemagne was king of the Franks who, earlier in the 8th century, conquered Germany and France.

### Chinese China

The **Imperial Silver Collection** is housed in one of the cupola-capped wings of St Michael's Gate facing Schauflergasse. Apart from the silverware used by Empress Elisabeth while at sea, the displays are mainly of Meissen tableware (1775), Sèvres and Minton porcelain and a magnificent 30m (98ft) table with gilded bronze centrepiece laid with porcelain vessels, figurines and a stunning gilded bronze centrepiece. Emperor Maximilian of Mexico's Chinese dinner service is also here in all its celestial intricacy and large enough to have fed a terracotta tomb army.

**Above:** *Ancient Swiss Gate in the Hofburg Palace.*
**Opposite:** *Fiaker cab drivers often colour-match the cab's wheels and upholstery with the horses' ear-muffs.*

### Spanish Riding School ★★★

You will often hear a student opera singer or musician playing in the lofty portals of St Michael's Gate. The shop inside will tell you about the **Lipizzaner horses** of the Spanish Riding School and the museum. The stalls for 65 of the highly trained white horses are just behind St Michael's Church, on the corner of Habsburgergasse and Reitschulgasse. Go through the arch in the latter and you will come to the **equestrian monument** to Kaiser Joseph II on Josefsplatz, erected in 1541 by Gerardus Mercator, the Latinized name of Flemish cartographer Gerhard Kremer (1512–94), inventor of the revolutionary Mercator map projection. This heralds the magnificent Prunksaal, or **State Hall**, and **National Library**, architect Johann Bernhard Fischer von Erlach's masterpiece. He designed the Schönbrunn Palace and Karlskirche. The Baroque interior – all marble pillars, ceiling frescoes, statues, twirling staircases, balconies, and wooden gilded bookcases – safeguards some 200,000 leather-bound books including a 15th-century Gutenberg Bible. Johannes Gutenberg (1398–1468) invented modern book printing, although the earliest known printed book, the *Diamond Sutra* (10th century), is in India. The huge library has some 2.5 million books, is 78m (85 yards) long and two storeys high. Long ladders help staff access books. The courtyard of the Prunksaal is where black marketeer Harry Lime wanted the military

**Above:** *Heldenplatz statue of Erzherzog Karl (archduke Karl) of Austria, who in 1809 was one of the few generals to defeat Napoleon.*
**Opposite:** Fiakers *wait their turn at the Albertina. The unpopular* War and Fascism *sculpture is on the right.*

authorities to believe he was run down by a truck in the 1949 film *The Third Man*.

### Hearts of Habsburg

The last section of the Hofburg is a wing linking the National Library to the Gothic church and monastery of **St Augustin**, with its lovely vaulting. Augustin (AD354–430) was bishop of ancient Hippo (in today's Algeria), one of the fathers of the Christian church. He was apparently something of a gallant in his youth and is credited with saying: '*Lord make me chaste … but not yet*'. En route to the dragon-slaying **St George's Chapel**, you pass through the little **Heart Crypt**, or Herzgrüftel, which houses 54 urns in polished silver containing, believe it or not, the hearts of Habsburg monarchs. Heart embalming and collecting was a macabre Habsburg habit they picked up in

Spain. The Augustinian church was a Habsburg wedding favourite and it has a long musical tradition: there's a full orchestra at Sunday high mass.

## Albertina ★★

The newly refurbished Albertina, the southernmost bastion of the Hofburg, not far from the opera, forms the final axis of the vast Imperial complex. It is a stunning **gallery of graphic art** and printed works: some 1.5 million including 65,000 water colours and drawings and 70,000 photographs. There are 145 drawings by Albrecht Dürer (1471–1528), the German master of apocalyptic wood cuts, and 43 by Raphael Santi (1483–1520), the Italian Renaissance painter and architect of today's St Peter's church in Rome. There are other works by Rembrandt, Klimt, Schiele, Leonardo, Breughel, Michelangelo, Rubens and Cézanne, not to mention the 20th-century Pablo Picasso, with his experimental and Cubist art.

After a thorough refit, the Albertina reopened in 2003. It is also the home of Vienna's **Film Museum** – actually a cinema.

## Palm House

The Palm House near the Albertina is not quite as grand as the out-of-town Schönbrunn greenhouses, but its café is gorgeous. Designed at the turn of the 19th century by Jugendstil architect Friedrich Ohmann, it looks like a London glass-and-girder railway station. The butterfly section has some 400 species in the humidity-regulated tropical environment for moths, birds and even bats. Butterflies,

### ADOLF'S ART

Austrian-born Adolf Hitler came to Vienna in 1907, aged 17, to be an artist. The judgement on his work by the Academy of Fine Arts was: 'inadequate'. From then on his book, *Mein Kampf* ('my struggle'), was to be directed against the Jews, Communists, Christians and practically everyone else. The sum of people who eventually died as a result of him was some 25 million. But it was not rejection that motivated him. Neither was he poor. He certainly had sufficient to go to the opera regularly. It's possible that Hitler's fits of rage, blame, depression, wild decisions and violence can be attributed to manic-depression at a time when there was no medication for the disease. Or possibly it was due to neuro-syphilis, only curable by penicillin which was only available in the medical armoury of his Anglo-American enemies.

**Below:** *Formal French gardens were all the rage in Vienna 250 years ago.*

in German *Schmetterling*, were supposed to steal milk or butter, hence their English name. The Palm House looks out onto the trees and lawns of the royal *Burggarten* and, some distance away, the lovely memorial to Mozart.

## The Gardens

There are the Imperial Gardens, or **Burggarten**, behind the Hofburg Palace, and for ordinary folk the **Volksgarten** in front where the old palace bastions used to be before Napoleon's cannon blasted them to pieces in 1809. Initially even the nobility preferred the formal French garden of the latter: a place to be seen and to scandalize. Gilded youth paid an entrance fee to the 'Aristocratic Corner.' Nowadays a rather dreary abandoned **Theseus Temple**, commissioned by a conciliatory Napoleon, provides a spot for students to sit and have a break. (Theseus conquered the Amazon ladies and married their queen, not unlike Napolean.)

In one corner of the Volksgarten there is a circular **lily pond**, **fountain** and formal **rose garden** with reputedly a thousand blooms, while in another is a seated **statue** of the **Kaiserin Elisabeth** or 'Sisi' looking mournfully over a

**Left:** *The Viennese love to spend lazy summer days at the Burggarten's Palm House.*

sunken **memorial garden**. Her cousin, 'Mad' King Ludwig of Bavaria, committed suicide, as did her only son Rudolf. On 10 September 1898 Elisabeth was stabbed to death for no apparent reason by Italian anarchist Luigi Luccheni as she was about to board a pleasure boat on Lake Geneva. Vienna lavishly mourned, but she had long been estranged from her emperor-husband. The garden also features a **monument** to the 19th-century playwright, **Franz Grillparzer**.

Ask a Viennese where the Volksgarten is and you may be directed to the outdoor 1950s nightspot overlooking the garden, Vienna's oldest club, or the equally wild Volksgarten Pavillon next door.

## DRUGS

Europe is a major consumer of narcotic drugs. The cartels are busily supplying the demand, Vienna being used periodically as a depot city. There is cocaine from South American and West African rings, cannabis from the Netherlands and heroin from Albania. This is the ugly face of the consumer society, but not as major a problem in Vienna as it is, for example, in London or Paris.

# 4
# Ringstrasse

In 1857, Kaiser Franz Josef I decided to get rid of the old medieval walls and build a horseshoe of 15 grand buildings facing onto a 4km (2.5 miles) long and 0.5km (0.3 mile) wide boulevard ring around the city. Construction took 30 years, and there are 15 epic buildings, all in the styles of bygone Classical, Gothic or Italian Renaissance glory.

## Rathaus ★★

The Rathaus spire makes this **Town Hall** look like a church with park, monuments, huge trees and drinking fountains in front. Its mind-boggling **Ceremonial Hall** is Austria's largest, with a pantheon of statues, gilt, stunning ostentation and lots of plaques of worthy burghers. A 3m (9ft) medieval knight in armour, the **Rathausman** as it is nicknamed, tops the tower at 102m (335ft).

The neo-Gothic Rathaus itself and the park in front have become a virtual fun park. There are free operas and concerts in summer and the **Christkindlmarkt**, or Infant Jesus market, for six weeks prior to Christmas.

## Burgtheater ★★

The **Imperial Court Theatre**, or Burgtheater, is a curved, bulbous building opened in 1888, the premier classic theatre of the German-speaking world at the time. Visibility was poor, acoustics worse and the Viennese were wont to say: 'In the Rathaus you see nothing (it was incredibly gloomy pre-electrification), in Parliament you hear nothing (not much democratic debate was

---

### Don't Miss

**★★★ MQ Museums**: there are dozens of them in the Museums Quartier.
**★★★ Kunsthistorisches Museum**: World's fourth largest art collection.
**★★ Parliament**: magnificent fountain and sculptures. Athena looks down from her golden crown.
**★★ Rathaus**: Christmas market.

---

**Opposite:** *The neo-classical architecture of Vienna's Parliament.*

## WALK THE CITY

Conducted by knowledgeable and professional Austrian guides, these tours can include the 1683 Turkish Siege, the Old City or the Homes of Mozart, Beethoven and Schubert. One of the most fascinating is the '1000 years of Jewish tradition'. Then there is *fin-de-siècle* Vienna and Sigmund Freud or Unknown Underground Vienna, or Vienna, Capital of Music. There are many others but only in German, French, Italian, Polish, Magyar or Spanish. *Queer Vienna*, advertised in pink, naturally is different. The tours are not expensive. Tel: (01) 774 8901. Website: www.wienguide.at

allowed), while in the Burgtheater you neither see nor hear'. Thirteen hundred people, surrounded by lofty boxes, galleries and frescoes, look down on a picture-frame stage. The grand claret-carpeted staircases in each wing, flanked by candelabras and busts of play-wrights, sweep up to a 60m (200ft) curved foyer. Post-performance, you can enjoy a coffee at the nearby **Café Landtmann**. Vienna's Sigmund Freud certainly did, usually with one of their famous *Guglhupf* cakes.

## Parliament **

**Athena**, mythical Goddess of Wisdom, in golden helmet stands high above a fountain of huge mermen and naked frolickers outside Austria's **Parliament** on

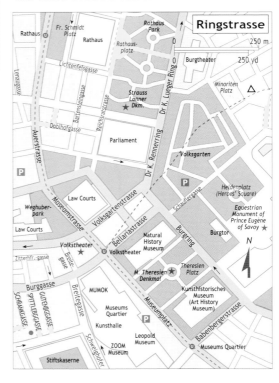

**Above:** *Athena, Goddess of Wisdom, stands over Parliament's fountain.*

the Ringstrasse. She and the 76 bronze chariots and classical skyline statues best seen from the sides are staggeringly gigantic – dwarfing tour groups, the busy Ringstrasse traffic and the Volksgarten beyond.

## Around the Volkstheater

Royalty had its Burg or royal theatre so naturally the people had to have a Volks or people's **theatre**. Walk up the side of the theatre on Burggasse and on the corner of Breitegasse you will see a huge old fob watch hanging above, supposedly the **smallest house** in Vienna, home to watchmaker Friedrich Schmollgruber and built 130 years ago in 1872.

The historic cobbled **Spittelberg** pedestrian area a little further, on the right of Burggasse, has always been a Bohemian area of old houses, actors, artists, restaurants, craft shops and boutiques. It was a workers' suburb and at one time Vienna's Red Light district.

### DESIGNER SHOPPING

If it's designer gear you're after, then there are plenty of top shops in the old city including Gaxi Tastmann's traditional Austrian costumes, Resi Hammerer for coats, Meinl's for food delicacies, Rasper and Söhne for Augarten porcelain, Kochert for jewellery, EMI for classical CDs, and cool gear for younger shoppers along Judengasse. Shakespeare and Co. will satisfy sophisticated readers.

### Museums Quartier ★★★

The new Museums Quartier (or MQ) complex across the Burgring motorway is one of the world's largest centres of culture and the arts. It includes an **Architectural Museum**, **Museum of Modern Art** (MUMOK), the dance training centre of the **Tanzquartier Wien**, the **ZOOM** children's museum, the **Arts Hall**, math space and the **Leopold Museum** of Austrian art with more than 5000 works. The MQ complex sprawls in an elegant modern architectural weave over a huge area. In the Leopold Museum, there is the world's largest collection of Austrian artist Egon Schiele's works. He died at the age of 28.

The main courtyard, **Quartier 21**, of the Museums Quartier is becoming the cool locality to hang out: bars, restaurant, art bookshop, ice-cream vendors, music and students draped on every ledge, plus studios for young avant garde artists, and record shops and designer clothes boutiques. Much of the Museums Quartier is open 24 hours a day and the bars and cafés well into the early morning. The **Tobacco Museum**

#### HANG IN THERE, SPORTS FANS

There is ice-skating in winter, tobogganing in Vienna's many parks, cross-country skiing along the Prater. In summer there is plenty of jogging: Nordic walking on the Prater Hauptallee or a guided run every Tuesday and Thursday through Vienna's parks including warm-up and stretching exercises. There are clearly marked routes for mountain biking. One can opt for bungee-jumping, climbing, tennis, inline skating, riding, golf, or, at Schönbrunn Palace, swimming. Choose your sport and contact www.wien.info

contains 2500 exhibits. Tobacco was introduced to the West 500 years ago by Spanish and Portuguese seamen returning from the Caribbean.

### Kunsthistorisches Museum ★★★

The Kunsthistorisches Museum is an exact Italian neo-Renaissance twin of the Natural History Museum opposite. It houses the world's largest collection of Dutch artist **Pieter Breughel's** (1525–69) art. Apparently he used to dress up in peasant clothes to be able to mingle among poor country folk and paint his evocative canvases of their lifestyle.

There are galleries of **Rembrandt van Rijn** (1606–69), a huge collection of **Peter Paul Rubens** (1577–1640), **Jan Vermeer**, the British artist **Thomas Gainsborough**, **Hans Holbein**, **Joshua Reynolds**, **Titian** (1488–1576), **Veronese**, **Tintoretto**, **Raphael** (1483–1520), **Caravaggio** (1571–1610), **Velázquez**, **van Dyck** and an excellent German collection, the so-named 'Danube School' including **Albrecht Dürer** (1471–1528).

The museum with its 8000 works, of which only 800 are on display, is a gargantuan feast. It houses the world's fourth largest collection of art.

**Opposite:** *A restaurant inside the square of the Museums Quartier.*
**Left:** *The Kunsthistorisches Museum, gallery of art, faces the Natural History Museum.*

# 5
# Karlsplatz

Three hundred years ago the Portuguese word for a rough pearl was *burroco*, hence Baroque, a style of decoration and architecture characterized by excessive ornamentation. Any corner, ceiling, wall or altar left bare was, it seemed, an affront to God. The style flourished in Europe from about 1580 to 1720.

It certainly hits you between the eyes when you walk into a church like **Karlskirche**. Inside, the magnificent dome's windows bathe the church in light, and a glass elevator rising to 47m (154ft) – when restoration is not in progress – enables one to see the beautiful fresco and artistry of Johann Michael Rottmayer. The whole complex towers over Karlsplatz and is particularly stunning from the little garden in front, or washed in pale aquamarine light at night.

## Karlsplatz

This sprawling square used to be a huge *nasch*, or sweet morsels, market. Today it is pure mayhem, a cats' cradle of wannabe Formula One cars, noise and seemingly suicidal pedestrians. Underground there are long multi-exit walkways lined with snack bars and news stands leading to the various U-Bahnen. The crowded tunnels are a favourite meeting place for young beer drinkers and recreational junkies.

The gents' loo exit near the opera is a riot of colour. It is decorated like an opera house complete with coloured lights and sopranos singing. As they say in Vienna, opera is everywhere.

### DON'T MISS

★★★ **Karlskirche**: Baroque dome, majestic interior.
★★★ **Naschmarkt**: fruit, vegetables, spices and fish.
★★★ **Staatsoper**: opera houses and classical music.
★★ **Russian Heroes' Monument**: Schwarzenbergplatz.
★★ **Stadtpark**: Strauss monument, Jugendstil pavilions.

**Opposite:** *White marble and copper roofs decorate Karlsplatz's old subway exit pavilions.*

In 1918, with the collapse of the monarchy, the Court Furniture Store that housed the imperial family furniture (including furniture they no longer wanted or furniture only used where they were in residence) had over half a million items and no Kaiser or queen to commandeer them. So they turned the storeroom into a museum and occasionally lent furniture out to movie-makers for films such as the 1950s *Forever My Love* on Empress Sisi. Period rooms have been completely reconstructed, including Crown Prince Rudolf's opium den.

## Marvellous Musikverein

The magnificent gilded Great Hall of the Musikverein Crescent Palace is home to the world-famous **Vienna Philharmonic Orchestra**. Their New Year's Day concert is seen worldwide by 1.3 billion TV viewers. The Hall can seat 1750 people. Its opulence is unsurpassed and its acoustics the world's best.

## Karlsplatz Station

Otto Wagner (1841–1918) was the Jugendstil architect of the new and the modern in the late 19th century. His highly colourful buildings are all over Vienna. He designed the Stadtbahn railway system (including 36 stations) and bridges. The jewel in his crown is the former Karlsplatz Station exit pavilions near the church, with their shimmering oyster-green, gilt and sunflower motifs. One is now a café. Green metal girders support slabs of white woven Italian Carrara marble, the marble used by Michelangelo to create his famous *David* in Florence 400 years earlier.

## Golden Cabbage Head

The 1898 Secession Art Gallery, named after Vienna's modern, or Jugendstil, art movement and nicknamed

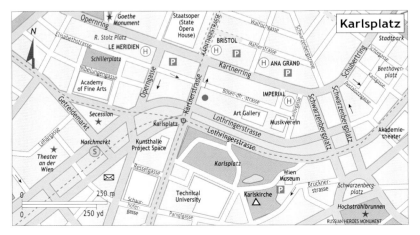

Golden Cabbage Head, has a dome, or rather a bees nest, of golden laurel leaves. Beneath it are the words: 'To each its art, to art its freedom.' And you have to be pretty arty to appreciate the symbolism of Gustav Klimt's frieze of Beethoven inside. Based on his 9th Symphony, its nude figure of Beethoven and bare walls got a pretty frigid reception when it was first displayed in 1902. Outside is a bronze (clothed) statue of Shakespeare's **Mark Antony**, replete and obese in his chariot pulled by a pride of (presumably Cleopatra's) desert lions. The **Secessionists** broke away from the mainstream **Austrian Artist's Association** in 1897 to form their own coterie, free of the copycat historicism that, for example, dominates the buildings of the Ringstrasse.

## Naschmarkt ★★★

There are midweek and Saturday food markets all over Vienna's suburbs but the biggest and the busiest is the **Naschmarkt** just off Karlsplatz. Its long avenue of stalls and eateries is packed with folk hunting fruit, spices, fish, cheese and 'deli' offerings.

In this harlequin village you can choose from 100 varieties of cheese, a Pandora's display of Persian spices, Slav nibbles, Viennese wines, Chinese take-aways, Turkish fish and a mesmerizing array of goodies. It is also a **Saturday flea market** of Indian silks, T-shirts, leather goods, jewellery, furs, dubious Russian icons,

### CROWN PRINCE

Hunting and mistresses are the sport of European princes. One such was Kaiser Franz Josef's son, Prince Rudolf. He fought with his father, couldn't abide his wife, thought he had a venereal disease and hadn't provided a male heir to the throne, so on 29 January 1889, at Mayerling near Baden, he committed suicide. The trouble was, he talked his latest mistress, 17-year-old Baroness Maria Vetsera, into doing likewise. The good news is that their story has become, in Vienna, as cherished as Romeo and Juliet and that of Rudolf's parents, Sisi and Franz Josef.

**Right:** *Dates and sweet-meats, fruit and fish to shatter any diet at the Bohemian Naschmarkt.*
**Opposite:** *Vienna's State Opera House facing frantic Opernring Street. Pavarotti and all the greats of the European opera world have sung here.*

## IMPERIAL HOTEL

Doffing top hat, the green-and-black jacketed concierge ushers you in. The foyer is dazzling in its fretted wood, marble, chandeliers, gilt and hint of cigar smoke. Built in 1863 as a city residence or *palais* for the Duke of Württenberg, it was sold, converted into a luxury hotel and opened by the Emperor Franz Josef in 1873. Its guest list of kings and presidents and film stars is unequalled. Hitler stayed here in 1938, as did Mussolini in 1943, hussled in through the back door having been rescued from Italian partisans. Outside, it faces a huge avenue of Elysian Field lime trees along the Ringstrasse. The Baroque *Fürsten* suite is all blue and gold, with palms, chaise longues, period furniture, chandeliers, massive drapes, Persian rugs and mirrors. If you need to ask the price, you can't afford it (actually, it costs €4,500 a night).

porcelain, tin toys, antique watches and 'Roman' coins. You will see every nationality, hear every language. Come Christmas Eve, a light snow falling, everyone is your friend as the mulled wine mellows into *Gemütlichkeit*.

### Staatsoper ★★★

Vienna has always been a world-renowned centre of western classical music and **opera**. Franz Schubert, Brahms, Bruckner, Josef Haydn, Mozart, Beethoven and Mahler spent long periods composing and playing in Vienna. Classical music resonates in western man's consciousness; we may not recognize the piece of music, but somehow we can hum the tune.

The **Opera House**, when it was first opened in 1869 as the first grand building of the emperor's Ringstrasse project, was not particularly impressive. The Kaiser said so, too. Consequently Edward van der Nüll, co-architect, hanged himself.

The **Volksoper** in Währingerstrasse is less expensive and specializes in lighter all-join-in **operetta**.

### Russian Heroes' Monument

An almost continuous rainbow hovers over the high jet fountain, or **Hochstrahlbrunnen**, at the open southern end of Schwarzenbergplatz which was built in 1873 to applaud Emperor Franz Josef's new city mains water system. Facing it and the elegant 1912 Art Nouveau **French Embassy**, is the massive shield of the **Russian Heroes Monument**, or *Russen Heldendenkmal*. A huge unknown Soviet soldier stands, gun-slung and gilt-helmeted, gazing across the frozen Steppe at the memory of some 16,000 Russians killed 'liberating' Vienna in 1945.

It is not a popular monument in Vienna, where it is less forgivingly known as the Monument to the Unknown Rapist. Some 90,000 women in Vienna were raped by Soviet troops.

## Stadtpark

You can still walk along the old **River Wien** as it cuts through Vienna's **Stadtpark** off Parkring. Largest of the green lungs that surround the Inner City, the park's main claim to fame is the 1925 **Strauss monument**. Depicting the larger-than-life Waltz King, violin in hand and gilded from head to toe, it is framed by an arch of naked river nymphs playing musical chairs.

### STREET MUSIC

There is a long tradition in Vienna of *Strassenmusik*. This is not at all like busking on the London Underground. You will see a student playing the cello in a Hofburg portal, or another, with her own backing on tape, singing opera. An elderly man in a little Alpine hat and tweed overcoat plays a violin, a jolly fellow in Am Hof market, a trumpet. They pop up everywhere. After all, this is the City of Music. And they are very good. Be generous: one may be a Strauss or Mozart one day.

# 6. Secrets of the Suburbs

Possibly the most intriguing address off shop-to-drop Mariahilfer Strasse is Number 28 Stumpergasse. It was here that young **Adolf Hitler** lived when he first came to Vienna in 1907.

'Never forget', *Niemals Vergessen*, reads today's chunky memorial slab from Mauthausen Concentration Camp outside the former Métropole Hotel (now Leopold-Figl-Hof) in Morzinplatz, former **Gestapo HQ**.

Neither Hitler's apartment, nor his favourite Café Sperl – or the Neue Burg Balcony at Heldenplatz where he announced the Anschluss or the grand Hotel Impérial where he stayed that fateful night – has any indication that he was there. There are no furled flags like every other historic building, no plaques, no mention in tourist literature.

## The Third Man Museum ★

Vienna was in ruins, rubble on every street, and Stephansdom all but razed to the ground. Electricity was intermittent, water pipes had burst, there were long queues for bread. The hospitals were barely working and no one trusted his neighbour. Vienna, having been ransacked by the Soviet army, was now ruled by the four victorious allies – USA, France, UK and Russia. Out of the sewers came *The Third Man*, Orson Welles, to make a fast buck with watered-down penicillin.

You can still visit several of the places where this film was made and if you are an addict, as many are, then go to **The Third Man Museum** in Pressgasse 25,

---

**DON'T MISS**

★★★ **Spittalau**: multi-mosaic smokestack of modern art.
★★ **Hundertwasser House**: sunburst of psychedelic colour.
★★ **Liechtenstein**: Austrian Biedermeier paintings.
★★ **Hitler's apartment**: art student, age 17.
★ **The Third Man Museum**: evocative zither music.

---

**Opposite:** *Hectic bustling along Mariahilferstrasse.*

**Right:** *The pre-World War II home where Sigmund Freud, the famous first psychologist, lived is now a museum on his life.*

## DOCTOR AND DRAMATIST

Described as the literary counterpart to fellow doctor Sigmund Freud, Arthur Schnitzler, born in 1862, also specialized in psychology. His writings focused on suppressed eroticism, anti-Semitism and the double standards of the bourgeois society in which he lived. His play *Der Reigen*, or *Dance in the Round*, explored the relationship between 10 couples. It shocked society and he was accused of writing pornography. He separated from his wife in 1921 but raised his two children. In 1928 his daughter Lili committed suicide.

Margareten's 5th district. Its eight rooms include composer Anton Karas's original zither (*see* panel, page 34).

## The Gorgeous Ones

**Neubau**, **Josefstadt** and **Alsergrund** form a third of the city's suburbs west and north of the **Innere Stadt**. Behind the Volkstheater, **Spittelberg** quarter's narrow cobbled streets hip-hop with life. Three hundred years ago this red light district (at the time) was frequented by the *Hübschlerinnen*, the 'gorgeous ones'. As in Amsterdam, they would preen at windows or tavern doorways, soliciting trade.

## Sigmund Freud Museum **

At Berggasse 19 you can see the house, now a museum, where Freud lived and the rooms in which he practised what would possibly have been considered, at the time, the 'dark art' of **psychoanalysis**. Between 1900 and 1910 Freud and others may have made Vienna the intellectual centre of the world, but Vienna knew it not. Most of **Freud's possessions**, including his famous couch, he took with him when he fled to London in 1938 to evade the Nazis. But you can see his coat, hat and walking stick, which he left, plus good reproductions of his work and home life. In 1896 Freud invented the word 'psychoanalysis' and in 1900 published his famous *The Interpretation of Dreams*.

Freud died in London a year after escaping the Nazis. He had been ill for many years; now it had become too much. His doctor, as agreed between them many years earlier, gave him a lethal dose of morphine.

## Liechtenstein Museum ★★

The Liechtensteins are a handsome pearls-and-polo couple who, through inheriting a little mountainous principality on the Rhine, have never really been short of a penny, except once in the 1960s when the family were forced to sell a Leonardo – to start a bank.

Fortunately for Vienna the family have been into art for generations. You can stroll through the picture-lined family rooms, admire Friedrich Wilhelm von Schadow's

**Left:** *The Liechtenstein's family house and art collection.*

**Right:** *Spittelau's paper rubbish incinerator and tower was given a spectacular refit by hippie architect Hundertwasser.*
**Opposite:** *Hundertwasser House, with its rainbow colours and verandah greenery.*

stunning Biedermeier portrait of young Schadow, smile at Peter Fendi's peeping servant girl and buy a package ticket that includes an audio guide, coffee and, quote, 'one piece of cake' in Rubens' Brasserie in the courtyard.

## Spittelau's Amazing Technicolour Dreamspire ★★★

If you stroll along the open walkway that links Spittelau Underground to the Economics University campus you will see, on your left and very close, is the huge chimney and building of the city's rubbish incinerator. But it is like no other on earth. In 1989 the ageing 'hippie' architect **Friedensreich Hundertwasser** was invited to turn a ghastly industrial blot into what it is today – a multi-coloured mosaic masterpiece not unlike an Aztec temple complete with soaring purple and gold smokestack joined in the middle by a huge gleaming bulb. For a city that rests on Baroque and Beethoven, this was not only far out, it was magnificently daring.

Hundertwasser, prince of peace, was a one-of-a-kind artist who was horrified by the flat, undecorated quick-build construction of our era. He thumbed his nose at the architectural establishment of the 1960s, gave speeches in the nude and was perhaps the best thing to happen to Vienna since Mozart shocked the music fraternity.

## Hundertwasser House ★★★

Competing with Spittelau is an **old apartment block** in Landstrasse which Hundertwasser also designed. It is an organic fantasy of uneven floor levels, mosaics, jazzy colours, rooftop gardens, cupolas, fountains, terraces, trees, pillars, funky lamps and statues, none of which synchronize in Hundertwasser's detestation of 'godless straight lines'. The result is one of the most picturesque and exciting buildings in Vienna, the darling of every tourist brochure. There is a '**toilet of modern art**' in the equally histrionic **souvenirs shopping village** where you can buy Mozart chocs and tourist T-shirts, and where the circular pub bar top has a stream running around it.

### PRATER

It was once a lush imperial hunting ground, then a kiss and cuddle spot for soldiers and pretty washergirls, and finally a park for poets to seek solace (*Indian Summer* by Adalbert Stifter). The Prater today, with the 100-year-old Ferris wheel (red wagons you can dine in), is a giant playground with 250 colourful, exciting music-whirled attractions. There are 14 car parks and 57 eateries.

## VIENNA WITH A VIEW

**Stephansdom Gothic steeple**: 553 steps to a panoramic view above the Inner City.
**Gloriette, Schönbrunn Castle**: Great sweep of lawn, fountain and forests to the distant city.
**Ferris wheel**: Prater funfair. As the sun goes down over the far Vienna Woods, the fair's lights sparkle below.
**Freud's dream Bellevue Heights**: at 388m (424yd), a grassy hilltop meadow where Sigmund Freud had a dream about the secret of dreams.
**Danube cruise from Krems to Melk**: unbelievable river gorges, vineyards and mountain castles.

If it all drives you to distraction, as it initially did the tenants in their 52 apartments, being continually asked to show visitors around their flats, don't worry: there is a resident psychotherapist on the premises.

## Red Vienna

After World War I, which saw an end to many tsars and emperors, Vienna's orientation was Marxist. Huge housing estates were built for the working masses in Vienna's suburbs to replace their unsanitary tenements. These, it was hoped, would assist the emergence of the 'new people' of the socialist Valhalla. There were health clinics, co-op shops, pharmacies, post offices, libraries, kindergartens, laundries, lots of green spaces and even communal bathing houses. One-tenth of the city's population was in this way provided with housing. Such housing is all over Vienna. But the most illustrious is the **Karl-Marx-Hof** in

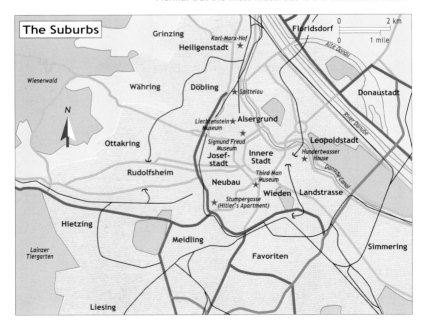

**Left:** *Karl-Marx-Hof: socialist apartments for the people.*

Heiligenstadt, built right alongside the railway and painted red. It originally consisted of 1325 flats. Karl-Marx-Hof suffered devastating artillery fire during the 1934 three-day Civil War when it was the bastion of resistance to the Austro-Fascist government. Some 2000 members of the socialist workers' militia were killed.

During 1923–34 a total of 63,736 apartments, 398 blocks, were built all over Vienna.

## MEET THE VOLK

Viennese are no more German than the Irish are English. One in three Viennese buy a newspaper and everyone loves lying on the sunny green banks of the Danube. The Viennese, even in a traffic accident, are soft-spoken; there's no feeling of big-city aggression and everyone is honest to a fault. Folk on the U-Bahn are better at pretending not to look at you than in other European cities. Menial jobs are mainly done by immigrants from Eastern Europe.

# 7
# Power and Glory

The sheer sweep of the emerald-green gardens, palace, Neptune Fountain, squares of clipped hedges, Gloriette folly, botanical gardens, Palm House, zoo and fringing woodlands have made **Schönbrunn**, the Habsburg Summer Palace, Vienna's most popular visitor attraction after the Hofburg. The grounds are larger than the state of Monaco.

## Hunter's Spring
The actual spring after which Schönbrunn is named is tucked away in the southeast of the complex between the Obelisk and Roman ruins paths. Folklore tells us that **Emperor Maximilian II** (1564–76) was out hunting far from Vienna when he discovered and rested at a spring. Later, he built a hunting lodge at a nearby watermill. Today the seated nymph Egeria, mythical 17th-century consultant to the king of Rome, pours the delightful water from her urn into a giant clam shell.

The spring was the Habsburgs' main source of drinking water, delivered to the palace by teams of mules, until in the late 19th century it was replaced by an Alpine alternative, Vienna's water of today.

## Baroque Palaces
It was not only the Catholic Church that used massive buildings to impress. In the 17th century, kings and emperors competed with one another to build great Baroque palaces. It was all vanity, of course, but it did leave some rather amazing buildings for posterity

### DON'T MISS

**\*\*\* Schönbrunn Gardens**: 1500 palatial rooms.
**\*\*\* Neptune Fountain**: sparkling opulence.
**\*\*\* Gloriette**: vast sculptures, vast views.
**\*\*\* Great Gallery**: ceiling frescoes, incredible opulence.
**\*\* Tiergarten**: Europe's first zoo.

**Opposite:** *The formal gardens of Schönbrunn belie the fascinating variety of the palace's museums and apartments.*

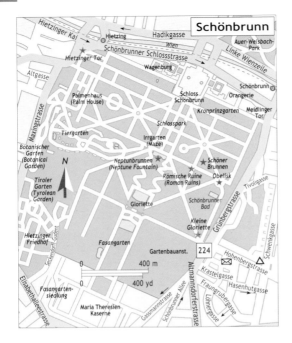

Schönbrunn

through our cameras. Schönbrunn was not to be a Versailles, merely a small palace of 1441 rooms, halls and possibly an equal number of staff to serve royalty's occasional needs. It would be over 50 years before the palace fully emerged as it is today.

### Schönbrunn Palace ★★★
The Grand Tour ticket will take you into the 40 rooms that are open to the public. These include **Maria Theresia's bedroom**, as well as the **Porcelain Room**, **Blue Chinese Salon**, **Napoleon Room** and the **Millions Room**, which got its name because it is said the Kaiserin paid in excess of a million silver florins to have it done up to her liking.

**Franz Josef's bedroom** is where he died on 21 November 1916. His sombre **study** is next door. The bedroom where Princess Elisabeth, Sisi, supposedly evaded her husband for two nights after their wedding is decorated in blue upholstery.

The 'English' flushing **toilet**, the first of its kind in the palace, is next door.

### The Virgin Queen
Empress **Maria Theresia** was known as the Virgin Queen. However, to her surprise she had 16 children, nine of whom survived to adulthood. Her youngest daughter was **Marie Antoinette** who, as the wife of **Louis XVI** of France, followed him to the guillotine in 1793 during the French Revolution. Her room is next

door to the nursery, both of which have the original décor from Maria Theresia's time.

## The Great Gallery ★★★

This is the most sumptuous gallery of all. Banks of **chandeliers** line each wall, illuminating the glass porticos in this enormous gold and white room. Giant **frescoes**, fretted and framed, look down from the ceiling in celebration of Habsburg glories.

The Napoleonic conflict ended rather disappointingly for the little Corsican who, in happier times, had twice stayed at Schönbrunn. The Great Gallery was used as an alternative ballroom during the Congress of Vienna in 1815, when Europe's high and mighty came together for nine months to discuss the future after Napoleon finally met his Waterloo. The rather cynical Viennese saying at the time was that there was lots of dance but little advance.

## Secret Meetings

Empress Maria Theresia apparently held secret meetings with Chancellor Count Wenzel von Kaunitz to discuss strategy and diplomacy during the Seven Years' War with Prussia that ended up involving half of Europe.

### NAZI HUNTER

Simon Wiesanthal survived the Nazi Holocaust. Three times he attempted suicide to avoid torture at Gestapo headquarters. He ended up in Mauthausen death camp in Austria and on 5 May 1945 was freed by US troops. His wife Cyla also miraculously survived. In 1947 he launched his Documentation Centre in Vienna, tracking down some 2000 former Nazis including Adolf Eichmann, an Austrian and the chief of the notorious SS (*Schutzstaffel*), who had vanished to Argentina from where the Israeli Secret Service, Mossad, abducted him, brought him to Israel, tried and hanged him in 1961, 16 years after his escape.

**Below:** *The Great Gallery at Schönbrunn has hosted kings and presidents.*

## STEPHANSDOM BELLS

Europe's second largest church bell after Cologne Cathedral is housed in the North Tower of Stephansdom (see page 39). It is known for its resonance as the *Pummerin*, or 'Boomer'. The first *Pummerin*, weighing 22,500kg (49,613 lb) and cast from Turkish cannonballs in 1711, was destroyed in the World War II fire that ravaged the cathedral. The new bell, hoisted in 1957, weighs a mere 21,383kg (47,150 lb) and is decorated with Turkish siege and 1945 fire scenes. Part of the inscription reads: 'Burst apart in the white heat of conflagration, I fell as the city moaned under the burden of war and fear'. Stephansdom has a total of 11 bells.

From his apartments in the Schönbrunn Palace, Kaunitz could apparently reach the **Round Chinese Room** via a secret spiral staircase hidden behind the panelling.

Maria, like Kaunitz, was a renowned foodie. She had a table made that would emerge from the floor laden with goodies. That way she and Kaunitz could tuck in and plan the downfall of their enemies without servants eavesdropping.

### Gloriette ★★★

In many ways the best way to see and explore Schönbrunn is not to begin with the palace itself but to head for the hilltop **Gloriette**, a high arched folly with a pond at its base. Stark against the horizon, it overlooks the whole sweep of the park and the city beyond. This is where Fischer von Erlach had intended building Austria's Versailles. But money was tight and there were more wars to fight. The stairs up to the central section and observation terrace are lined with delicious monsters, convoluted sculptures whose meaning may have been lost even to their creator. On the same side as the **Tyrolean Garden** and loos, there is a 'Sound of Music' **Lederhosen Café**

with great views at the windows.

The surrounding **woods** with their paths, benches and cool dappled sunlight – the walk up to the Gloriette is steep in parts – are a good place to picnic and distance oneself from the madding crowd.

### Neptune Fountain ★★★

Neptune was the Roman god of the sea. What better name therefore to give to Schönbrunn's fabulous fountain? It divides the palace gardens in two with its splendid symphony of ascending sea horses, porpoises, fish, seashells, fountains and a motley crew of muscular gods and their lissom surf ladies – and, of course, old deep-water Neptune himself.

## Palm House

The graceful, undulating glass-and-iron **Palm House** takes its cue, so to speak, from Kew Gardens in London. It is separated into three climatic zones. Viennese tourism folk will tell you it is the largest Palm House in the world. At 113m (371ft) long with

45,000 panes of glass, it possibly is. It certainly was when built in 1882. It is awash in a riot of tropical flowers and palms, some 100 years old.

The **Desert House** next door has Wild West cacti and all manner of geckos and creatures of the dunes.

## Wagenburg

In horse-drawn days, carriages were equivalent to today's Mercedes. The **Wagenburg** (**Museum of Carriages**) lies to the side of the main palace. The super-limo is the **coronation carriage** of Maria Theresia's husband, Franz Stephan. Weighing in at a cool 4000kg (8820lb), this stretched beast is a fantasy in gold plate, painted panels, twirls, bobs and windows of the finest Venetian glass. The royals used to have it completely taken apart, packed and sent off to far corners of the empire for reassembling whenever a cousin was crowned or got married.

At Schönbrunn there is a large zoo, the **Tiergarten**, with 750 animals.

**Above:** *Neptune's wild and wonderful fountain at Schönbrunn.*
**Opposite:** *Neptune Fountain in the centre and forest to the left and right lead up to the Gloriette at Schönbrunn Palace.*

### THIMBLE TIME

The world's oldest Clock Museum, or Uhrenmuseum, can be found in Schulhof Street in the Baroque Obizzi Palace. Its fascinating exhibits include a pendulum clock that will take 21,000 years to complete a single revolution. The delightful Doll and Toy Museum is next door.

# 8
# Gardens of Green

Not since the ancient Egyptians has anyone done death like the Viennese. Funerals have always been an opportunity for pomp, circumstance and a beautiful corpse, *eine schöne Leich*. Or, as the **Undertaker's Museum** in Wieden will testify, a 'decent' burial. The **Central Cemetery** (Zentralfriedhof) in Simmering is huge, Europe's second largest with 3.3 million residents in its tree-lined red-lanterned graves, memorials and exotic pantheons in an area of 2.5km$^2$ (1 sq mile). The cemetery was opened in 1874, replacing the five municipal cemeteries, and ever since has been a place to stroll, tend family graves, pray, water the flowers, chat and picnic.

## Zentralfriedhof ★★

The huge Jugendstil main gate, Tor No. 2, at Zentralfriedhof, with its soft drink stands and flower stalls, leads down past the 500 **Tombs of Honour**, or Erengräber, where you can walk with the immortals. Mozart, Ludwig van Beethoven – 26,000 mourners attended Beethoven's funeral – Franz Schubert, Gluck, Brahms, Hugo Wolf and Josef Lanner are here: all the king's men and all the Strausses.

There are ten-foot-high angel-weeping, despairing-wife sculpted tombs of the wealthy bourgeoisie (Group 14A) whose progeny patently had deep-pocket inheritances, albeit little taste. Look out for the comedy-tragedy tomb of actor Curt Jurgens (the sealed photo on his tomb shows him as an SS officer, a role he played) and the unusual ice-pick monument to the Austrian

## Don't Miss

**★★★ Vienna Woods:** unsurpassed forested wilderness.
**★★ Zentralfriedhof:** huge sculptured gravestones.
**★★ Belvedere Palaces:** sphinxes and gardens.
**★★ Mozart's Grave:** birdsong and greenery.
**★ Nameless Ones:** Danube's forgotten suicides.

**Opposite:** *A mountain fell, they say, when the young Mozart died in 1791.*

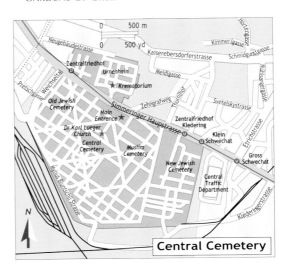

Central Cemetery

climbing expedition lost last century in the Himalaya.
In Group 33F Row 1/1 is the grave of Dominik Bauer
(1841–1904), the cemetery's first grave digger.

### Unknown Soldiers

Beyond the bulky church is the **Soviet War Cemetery**,
with two huge helmet-in-hands soldiers guarding the
many graves of those killed in their attack on Vienna at
the end of World War II. The World War I memorial is
a powerful depiction of a distraught mother weeping
over her dead sons. The paupers' section has no trees,
the little wooden crosses already falling over, but fresh
flowers lie there.

On the opposite side of the road to the cemetery are
two **restaurants**. One, a beer garden, sells mackerel
fillets from Slovenia and Winzer Krems wine. After a
morning in the Friedhof you'll probably need both.

### Palaces of Delights

On a sloping piece of ground south of the inner city,
there is a magnificent series of formal French gardens
and two huge Baroque palaces. The lower is a resi-

dence, and the upper is a 'palace of delights' built for French-born **Prince Eugène of Savoy**, Viennese military hero who defeated the Turks in 1683.

Gazing over this vast landscape of manicured hedges, lawns, flowerbeds, rows of classical statues, ponds, fountains and the two massive green-topped palaces with their patios and portals, one wonders where on earth the money came from. In fact it came from Eugène's share of the booty from the Turkish campaign which he only received 31 years after the victory.

### The Lower Belvedere ★★

The **Museum of Austrian Baroque Art** is housed here, and in what is called the Orangerie (used to protect plants in winter) is the **Museum of Austrian Medieval Art**. The **Hall of Grotesques** boasts grimacing faces not unlike the female sphinxes that adorn the paths between the lower and upper cascades in the gardens. The **Marmorsaal**, or Marble Hall, is a paean of lavish praise to Eugène in which he even features, somewhat sycophantically, as the god Apollo.

Four squares of gardens and huge-hedged hideaways separate Lower Belvedere from the impressive, mightily sculpted **Lower Cascade** that marks the beginning of the **Upper Belvedere Gardens**. However, the gravelled pathways, imperial ostentation and sombre symmetry lack a human touch. The people who inhabited these incredible palaces were undoubtedly a world apart from ordinary Viennese folk.

**MASTER OF DIALECT**

There is a square and an underground station named after Johann Nepomuk Nestroy. Born in 1801, he wrote 83 plays and was famous for his mastery of the Viennese dialect, folk tradition and Viennese popular theatre. He also had an acerbic wit and often had to skirt around the censors and all-powerful Minister Metternich to get parody and criticism on stage, always covering it with a veil of comedy.

**Left:** *Grand grieving tomb architecture is a feature of the Central Cemetery.*

## UNDERGROUND

You can get to practically
anywhere you want to on
Vienna's U-Bahn, or
Underground, plus a little
walking. The U-Bahn system
has a total length of 65,6km
(41 miles) with 35,1km (22
miles) of tracks underground.
There are 81 stations. The
line with the most passengers
is the one from Karlsplatz to
Stephansplatz: 167,000
passengers daily. The longest
nonstop tunnel is 9,39km
(5.9 miles) long and the
average distance between
stations is 771m (843yd).

## The Upper Belvedere ★★

This palace is stark and solid, particularly when viewed
from the main entrance, with its black filigree iron
gates, ponds and formal gardens. It was purpose built
for a military man and for the popular masked balls of
the time with plenty of open space for fireworks displays. It is much larger than its sister palace down
below. In this palace's **Marble Hall**, the Austrian State
Treaty of 1955 was signed, granting the country full
independence after 10 years of occupation by the
World War II Allies. The Hall contains a wonderful collection of Austria's three great Jugendstil modernist
painters, Klimt, Schiele and Kokoschka. Here you will
see Klimt's most photographed work, the yellow-gold
and superbly colourful *The Kiss*, behind glass. It is of
himself and his lady, Emilie Flöge.

Near the entrance gates to the Upper Belvedere is the
**Alpine Garden**. It was started in 1803, Europe's oldest. It
leads into the university's even older **Botanical Garden**
flanking the Belvedere.

## Heeresgeschichtliches Museum

This museum, the first public museum in Vienna,
opened in 1856. It formed part of the vast **Barracks** and
**Arsenal** the emperor decided was wise to establish on
high ground near the new Ringstrasse. Built in neo-

Byzantine cum crusader fort style, it was originally four chunky red brick barracks, of which only the arsenal and museum remain.

It covers the last 500 years of European warfare. The blood-stained tunic and vintage Gräf & Stift open car in which heir to the Austrian throne, Archduke Franz Ferdinand, and his wife Sophie were assassinated on 28 June 1914 is here. So are Napoleon's battle greatcoat and the magnificent uniforms which made Austria's soldiers shooting ducks – they were, however, peacock attractive at court balls.

**Naval Power** has a model of the U27 submarine which hunted and killed with the wolf pack against Atlantic convoys. Its commander was none other than *Sound of Music* captain, Georg Ritter von Trapp.

**Above:** *Lake and formal gardens lead from the filigree entrance gates to the Upper Belvedere Palace.*

### Mozart's Grave ★★

On 5 December 1791, possibly the world's greatest and most loved composer, **Wolfgang Amadeus Mozart**, died. The 35-year-old music genius had been suffering for two weeks from rheumatic fever.

**Right:** *Lilac blossom and wild flowers provide a carpet of honour to Mozart's grave.*

Plague was a concern in Vienna at the time so Mozart's body was covered with lime, placed in a sack and lowered into a cheap **mass grave**. This was a common practice at the time for everyone except the seriously rich. Fifty-two years after Mozart's death, his widow **Constanze**, now an old woman, tried to find her husband's grave. But mass graves, as was the custom, were emptied every eight years.

### The Nameless Ones Cemetery ★

The Undertaker's Museum has a cord and bell device that could be rung from inside your grave if you felt you were not quite dead. But there was no such luck for those buried in the Nameless Ones Cemetery, **Friedhof der Namenlosen**, near the waters of the Alberner Harbour, on the southern outskirts of the city. One hundred years ago, the swirling waters of the river curved and twisted here, throwing up a grizzly harvest of bodies: men, women and children who had committed suicide, were perhaps murdered or simply drowned – the lost nameless ones of the Danube. This is their last little graveyard.

It's a poignant, lonely spot with a Dickensian feel to it. There are 104 graves marked by iron crosses. A few have names but many are simply marked *Namenlos*, or Nameless. The graves are well tended, many with flowers. There is a pillbox **chapel**, a lovely poem etched on a plaque at the entrance and a slot in which to drop a coin or two for flowers.

## Lainzer Tiergarten

The Lainzer Tiergarten is not actually a zoo but a **game reserve** of boar, deer and wolves, 25km$^2$ (10 sq miles) in size, to the west of Hietzing. There are 80km (50 miles) of walking and cycling paths in the ancient oak and beech **forests**. No traffic is allowed and there are no formal gardens to pull in the crowds. The Lipizzaner horses of the Spanish Riding School spend the summer here when they are not performing their majestic leaps in the Hofburg. The **Hermes Villa** is a stroll away from the Main Gates. But this love nest in the woods, the emperor's gift to his wife to bribe her back to Vienna, didn't do the trick. Like Hermes, she was soon off again.

## Vienna Woods ★★★

The **Wienerwald**, or Vienna Woods, is a 1250km$^2$ (482-sq-mile) belt of forest, woodland meadows, hills and

### VIRTUAL INNOVATION

With goggles, high-intensity optical laser wand and a good imagination you can enter the 360-degree three-dimensional world of the Virtual Reality Theatre in the Technisches Museum not far from Schönbrunn's main gates (two showings daily). If you thought Vienna was all waltz and Sachertorte, the museum, recently transformed, innovative and state of the art (or rather science), proves otherwise. It offers strange phenomena, scientific mysteries, digital technology and high-voltage experiences. There is a mine, the oldest still working automobile (1875), heavy industry, music to lull you in the musical instruments section, and a treasure chest of vintage cars and bicycles in the popular transport collection.

**Left:** *The lonely cemetery of the Nameless Ones on the Danube.*

**Right:** *A fit cyclist pumps uphill near the Vienna Woods.*

### THE HILLS ARE ALIVE

The tail end of the Alps is only 90km (60m) south from Vienna. There are direct trains to Simmering whose historic railway was built in 1854. Weaving its way through 31 tunnels and viaducts and beautiful Alpine scenery, it is the first railway to be designated a UNESCO World Heritage Site. The three most popular mountains for both skiing and wandering are Rax, Schneeberg and Simmering. All three have year-round ski lifts. Rax at 2007m (6587ft) has a large 34km (21-mile) plateau, while Schneeberg at 2075m (6810ft) is southern Austria's highest peak. The chalets in the mountains all have stunning views and good restaurants, in particular the 1929 Looshaus in the Mount Rax area. For information, contact Tourismusregion Süd-alpin, tel: (02664) 2539-1, website: www.tiscover.com/noe-sued

streams surrounding Vienna, in an arc that stretches from the Kahlenberg hills on the Danube, right round the city's western suburbs to the foothills of Austria's southern Alps. Few cities have a green lung of this magnitude on their suburban doorstep.

### Grinzing

Heuriger wine-farm taverns decorate this winding medieval village with its colourful little houses. Nobel laureate **Albert Einstein**, German-born US physicist and mathematician who formulated the Theory of Relativity, stayed in Grinzing at No. 70 Grinzinger Strasse for four years (1927–31), not far from where **Beethoven** lodged in the summer of 1808 while composing his famous Pastoral Symphony.

At the top of the village is the **Beethovenhaus**, or Heuriger Mayer, where the composer stayed in 1817; it is a farmhouse with a long, vine-covered cobbled courtyard. The little **church of St James**, originally built in the 12th century, faces the **Parish Square** outside. The walk to the hilltop meadow of Bellevuehöhe, where the *Secret of Dreams* was revealed to **Sigmund Freud**, passes the old spired **church of the Grieving Mary** and rolling slopes of vines.

## Kahlenberg

This summit of 484m (1537ft) at the northeast edge of the Vienna Woods has a marvellous view over the whole of Vienna, the Danube and as far south as the Schneeberg Alps. **Kahlenberg** is one of two peaks, the other being the slightly lower **Leopoldsberg** (425m, 1350ft). These two hills changed names in 1693 and, to add to the confusion, Kahlenberg was originally called *Sauberg* after the plentiful wild boar found here.

## Klosterneuburg

The green Baroque dome of the **Augustinian monastery**, looking for all the world like a helmeted soldier with goggles, dominates the small village. This monastery on a hill overlooking the Danube – clearly visible from the train to Krems – dates back to the 12th century. It's placed on a spot, the story goes, where **Duke Leopold III** promised to found an abbey if he tracked down his wife's veil carried off in the wind. He was later canonized and in fact became the **patron saint of Austria**.

The **Sammlung Essl**, Austria's largest private art museum, is in Klosterneuburg, featuring post-1945 modern Austrian and international art.

### SWEETS FOR THE SWEET

A few drops of orange juice on crushed ice was Empress Elisabeth's idea of a meal. Nothing would dissuade her from a strict diet, except violet sherbet from Café Demel. What is good enough for a queen is good enough for a commoner. Similar dainties, candied violets, are still today one of Demel's mouth-watering specialities sold in period-piece boxes.

**Left:** *Heurigers sell the new wines made from their own vineyards.*

# 9
# Blue Danube

The Danube has long been tamed and divided by the Viennese into four rivers, using techniques similar to those employed in the construction of the Suez Canal. Now, climate change apart, there is relatively little risk of the flooding that raged in previous centuries.

Three bridges cross the sliver-island that separates the parallel **Danube** and **New Danube** rivers, leading to a series of urban riverside parks where the local folk swim at clubs, sail, fly kites and go boating at weekends. The New Danube, and its island built in the 1970s, has become Vienna's outdoor playground. There are restaurants, sports facilities, picnic areas, nudist bathing and 40km (25 miles) of beaches.

## Donau Park
The Donau Park occupies most of the middle section of the island between the **New Danube** and the **Old Danube**. Orientate yourself by walking from the Alte Donau metro (U1) towards the 252m (827ft) **Danube Radio Tower** with its two revolving restaurants and a viewing terrace reached by express lift. There are children's playgrounds and pony rides, peaceful lily-lakes, apocalyptic sculptures by Karl Wolf and banks of patterned flowers. The **Isola Beer Garden** sits at the foot of the huge tower.

## Copa Kagrana ★★
Kagram, not far east of Donau City, is a dull commuter suburb. Named after Rio de Janeiro's Copacabana

## Don't Miss

**★★★ Ferris wheel:** exciting views.
**★★ Wiener Kriminalmuseum:** dark secrets, dark murders.
**★★ Copa Kagrana:** Afro-Cuban revelry.
**★ Augarten:** Nazi flak towers.
**★ Donau-Auen National Park:** Napoleon headquartered his army here in 1809, ready to attack Vienna.

**Opposite:** *The giant Ferris wheel at the Prater Amusement Park has been thrilling visitors for over 100 years.*

**Right:** *Exotic Afro-Cuban eateries line Copa Kagrana's wild waterfront on the Danube.*

scimitar of surf and sand, Vienna's Copa Kagrana is a riverside stretch of restaurants, pulsating music and gilded youth. The smells and the samba waft over you as you sip a Caipirinha or Cuba Libre. Pretty waitresses in pampas sombreros and white cowboy boots call you to drink, the barman looks like a Colombian Capo and everyone is tapping to the thunder of the music.

### The Prater Amusement Park ★★★

In Vienna it is the **Riesenrad Giant Ferris Wheel** that defines the city skyline. The Prater amusement park, forests and recreation area in **Leopoldstadt** was opened to the public in 1766 (Prater means 'a plain'). There is jogging, horse-riding, a children's railway, trade fair centre, planetarium, racecourse, tennis clubs and the amusement park with its Ferris wheel made famous in *The Third Man* film.

The **great wheel**, designed by British military engineer Walter Basset, initially weighed in at 440 tonnes, with 120 spokes and 30 cars. You get taken 64m (210ft) off the ground, with the wheel revolving in a slight stagger at 75cm (29in) per second, the ride lasting 20 minutes. You can even book a formal evening dinner party in one of the cars.

The long, wide and shady **Hauptallee** (main avenue) is busy at weekends with hearty fellows and jogger-damsels in designer T-shirts, shades, iPods and ski-sticks. Branch left or right off the Hauptallee and you

---

### TINKER, TAILOR, SOLDIER, SAILOR

When Napoleon's armies were blasting away at Vienna's defences 200 years ago, there were no department stores to help the burghers stock up. There were market days, of course, with lots of noisy bargaining, but everything else more or less came to you: pretzel sellers, ink merchants, ribbon sellers (few women cut their hair), knife sharpeners, tinkers, ashmen to collect the previous night's ashes, and even water people selling from vast wooden barrels. Many would sing out their wares.

are immediately into forest, gardens, streams, occasional lakes and loads of wild flowers. Halfway down, near the loos, is a tiny open-bench tearoom, with 1950s music.

## Hitler's Final Solution

By 1910, a third of **Leopoldstadt** was Jewish: some 60,000 people, increasing to nearly 200,000 in the 1920s, a continuously changing population of the poorest of the poor. In the 1920s, Viennese writer **Joseph Roth** wrote, 'there is no harder lot than that of the Eastern Jews newly arrived in Vienna.' In World War II Hitler's **Nazis** once again made Leopoldstadt the Jewish ghetto. It was from here that many left for the extermination camps of their fellow Austrian

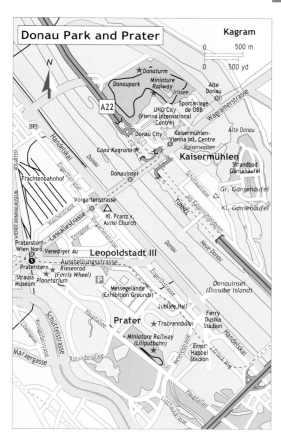

Nazi, **Karl Adolf Eichmann**. Plaques today in Leopoldstadt record locations from where Jews were rounded up.

## Augarten ★

Historically if not aesthetically attractive, Vienna's six monstrously huge **Flaktürme**, anti-aircraft towers, built by the Nazis nearly 70 years ago to ward off Allied bombing, are dotted around Vienna in three sets of two towers forming a huge triangle around Stephansdom. Each was con-

---

### 'OH TANNENBAUM'

The first *Tannenbaum*, or Christmas tree, only appeared in Vienna in 1814, possibly as a side-perk of the huge festivities going on at the Congress of Vienna in the Hofburg. Before that St Nikolaus brought children presents on 6 December.

structed of reinforced concrete 3m (10ft) thick and capable of housing 30,000 troops. They look like giant grey dice with jutting circular platforms necklacing the top. Their designer, highway architect **Friedrich Tamms**, thought that when the war was won the towers could be covered in black marble with the names of those who had died for the Führer carved in memorial gold.

The Augarten houses the **Vienna Porcelain Factory**, the second oldest in Europe after Meissen.

### Murder Most Foul

There is a **Torture Museum** in Vienna, an **Undertaker's** or **Death Museum** and a **Criminals Museum**. They are deliciously macabre and perhaps not to everyone's taste. But if you like murder, mayhem and detective fiction, then start with the small house of horrors, Wiener Kriminalmuseum.

### Wiener Kriminalmuseum ★★

The exhibits, often in darkened red silhouette, proceed blood-thirstily from century to century. There are lots of period pictures of knife-wielding felons and public executions, historic police uniforms, 'black' or illegal fishermen, the beginnings of forensic science and a reproduction of 'Instrument F', a sophisticated guillo-

**Right:** *Flaktürme, or anti-aircraft towers, were built in the Augarten Park to ward off World War II British bombers.*

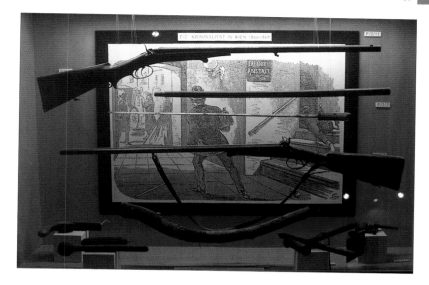

tine introduced to Vienna in 1938 by the Nazis. More than 1000 people were decapitated.

## Donau-Auen National Park ★

This 10,000ha (24,710-acre) national park includes the Lobau, a wooded region of cycling paths, riverside meadows, wilderness and a ring of lakes that do a sterling job of keeping the fringing suburbs of Aspern, Essling and Grosse Enzerdorf at bay. Some 5000 species of insects, butterflies, birds and other creatures are testimony to its unspoilt reaches, particularly for the more adventurous.

The **Lower Lobau** is where all four **Danube** watercourses finally merge to head for Bratislava and Budapest. It was here in the woods that **Napoleon** marshalled his armies in 1809, preparatory to attacking Vienna. The Austrians had withdrawn to these dark forests and took Napoleon by surprise in a quick victory that cost the French warlord 20,000 men. A monument in the forest marks **Napoleon's HQ**, his **powder magazine** and the **cemetery** where his soldiers are buried.

**Above:** *Murder weapons in the Wiener Kriminalmuseum are lit in blood red.*

### BAKER'S DOZEN

In medieval times there were rules about practically everything. Until about AD1400 Viennese bakers could not sell their delicious loaves from their bakeries. This had to be done from quickly erected stalls in today's smart Graben (Ditch) Street or in the Hoher Markt, the old Roman Forum. And of course a loaf of bread had to be exactly the right size. An indentation in the giant portals of St Stephan's Cathedral was used for measuring the loaves.

# 10
# Beyond Vienna

Deep in the bowels of the earth thermal hot springs bubble up all over the world to warm and ameliorate the many ailments that the flesh is heir to. **Baden**, 25km (19 miles) south of Vienna, is one such place. Compact and, in spite of a grandiose gambling casino, rather sleepy, the little town of Baden basks in its cute pastel assortment of neoclassical buildings linked by cobbled streets beneath the green Vienna Woods, hills and the Kurpark spa complex.

From 1804 onwards, **Ludwig van Beethoven** came here regularly each summer. Consequently there is a Beethoven Platz, a Beethovengasse and a Beethovenhaus (three small rooms) where the composer finished his Ninth Symphony.

The holiday air and bracing baths intrigued the composer. Dishevelled and with his mop of wild hair, he soon became known as a bit of an eccentric, disturbing the elderly burghers.

## BADEN

Baden may seem reserved but it has 'a past'. It was the setting for the 1870s novel *Venus im Pelze*, translated as *Venus in Fur*, by **Count Sacher-Masoch**, whose deviancy gave birth to the expression 'sadomasochism', a play on his name.

Up into the park, past avenues of trees, is a monument to the **Strauss** family surrounded in spring by banks of red tulips. The higher up the path you climb the better the view of both the spa and Baden.

### DON'T MISS

**\*\*\* Cruise on the Danube:** hilltop castles, villages, vineyards.
**\*\*\* Melk Monastery:** Baroque masterpiece, medieval village.
**\*\* Budapest:** by hydrofoil. Soviet Statue Park.

**Opposite:** *Waiters in waistcoats and long aprons: Baden café couture.*

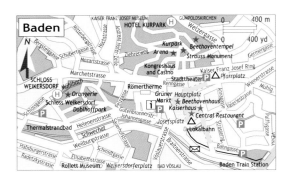

## Museums and Baths

**The Rollett Museum**, south of the Schwechat on Weikersdorfplatz, is a fanciful 1905 neo-Renaissance building housing a collection of death masks, skulls and 'arcanobilia'. The **Kaiser Franz Josef Museum** has arms, military uniforms, banknotes, penny-farthing bicycles and just about anything the local folk have managed to collect.

If you would like to take the waters, you can try the **Thermalstrandbad** on Helenenstrasse or the indoor **Römertherme**. **Doblhoffpark** nearby has formal gardens, an orangerie and woods. Not far from Baden is **Gumpoldskirchen**, a wine-growing area full of folksy Heurigen drinking spots.

The S-Bahn from Vienna's Südbahnhof station gets you to Baden.

## BURGENLAND

Rabbits and foxes run in and out of cover across the flat plains that eventually become Hungarian steppe, or *puszta*, stretching either side of the red bullet train as it glides across the **Burgenland**. You'll see wheatfields, dazzling yellow rape, massive windfarm windmills, and vapour trails in the high cold air. Occasionally there is a little wood, a village with spired church, and farms protected by sand barriers. Suddenly above the rolling vineyards appears a huge tower, McDonalds Supermac, blitzing one's vista of sleepy rural bliss.

---

### THE GREAT GAME

The 2008 UEFA European Football Championship, Euro 2008, took place in Austria and Switzerland. A total of 16 teams participated in the tournament. Austria and Switzerland automatically qualified as hosts, with Austria making its first appearance in the tournament. Ernst-Happel-Stadium with 53,000 seats is where the final took place. It is in the huge Prater recreation complex. A good many trees around the stadium had to be cut for security reasons. There were other stadiums, expanded and renovated for the event, in Salzburg and Innsbruck. Austria's Hypo-Arena in Carinthia Province was constructed specifically for Euro 2008.

Burgenland stretches over the whole of eastern Austria. It was stitched onto Austria in 1921 after the fall of the Habsburgs, and its population, like that of all borderlands, is a mix of Austrian and such minorities as Croatian, Hungarian and Roma (Gypsy).

The train from Vienna's Südbahnhof runs every hour and takes 45 minutes to the storybook station at **Neusiedl-am-See**, surrounded by vineyards. From there buses are infrequent. There is usually a taxi to take you through the small town to the resort shores of **Neusiedler Lake**, a huge, shallow (maximum 2m/6ft) lake covering 230km² (89m²) and dividing Austria from Hungary.

A long flat road leads down to holiday cottages and small hideaway marinas ending at a large seaside park dominated by Da Marco's huge three-storey thatched hotel-restaurant.

**Sailing** is the main summer activity on the lake. During the worst heat of summer (Vienna and surrounds are much hotter than most of western Europe), the water level can evaporate, dropping so low that you can walk across the lake. During winter it becomes a Breughel fairyland as it freezes into a huge ice-skating rink. This is when the ice sailors, in their fast boats,

### SMOKING IN VIENNA

'Smoking can kill you.' *'Rauchen kann tödlich sein.'* This warning is displayed on every packet of cigarettes in the world, but Vienna is reasonably smoking-friendly. All hotels have smoking and non-smoking rooms. There are no restaurants or cafés where you cannot smoke. Albeit, nearly all will have carefully demarcated areas. There are many tiny Tabak shops on almost every corner. In Vienna's Tobacco Museum, you can browse through 2500 objects and learn about nicotine and its history since the Spanish and Portuguese adventurers first brought the weed to Europe 500 years ago. To stamp out a cigar, incidentally, is not done. You should let it die of its own accord.

**Left:** *Bathtub for all-comers. Plaque on a bathhouse facing Baden's square.*

come down from Vienna. Ironically, when the winter winds blow the waves in, the shallow water can build up into minor tsunamis.

The lake's fringing reed beds – considered to be the world's best for weaving – are, of course, a wonderland for migratory birds, especially on the southeast shore, one of Austria's six national parks. Be sure to have your binoculars with you.

### Hell's Angels

When the sun shines on Neusiedler See, the **bikers** come out to play. A 50-bike battalion will arrive on their vintage ultraclassic Harleys: men and women in leathers, studs, steelworker boots and bandannas come here to relax, eat and dance in the wine-friendly tree'd gardens of Da Marco's alongside the old pier (or *mole*) where you can hire any manner of lake craft.

### Eisenstadt

The provincial capital of Burgenland is Eisenstadt where **Josef Haydn**, the composer, lived for 31 years as a personal musician to the aristocratic Hungarian Esterházy family. The family still owns the 14th-century

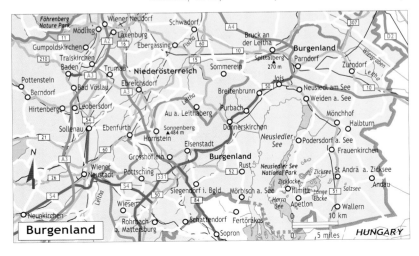

**Schloss**, a vast medieval fortress offering guided tours. Nearby is the old and well-preserved walled Jewish ghetto, **Unterberg**, and the **Austrian Jewish Museum**. All 446 of Unterberg's Jews were sent to death camps in 1938.

## CRUISING THE BLUE DANUBE

King **Richard I, the Lionheart** (Coeur de Lion) of England, who reigned from 1189–99, was a romantic knight errant in the poetic

Camelot days of Sherwood Forest and Robin Hood. Richard took the Cross in 1188 and went on the **Third Crusade**. He could be hot-tempered and made cutting remarks about Leopold of Austria and the Holy Roman Emperor's representative. Shipwrecked on his way home, he was obliged to go overland. He passed through Vienna, was recognized – kings are difficult to disguise – was captured and imprisoned for two years (1192–94) in a hilltop castle overlooking the village of **Dürnstein** on the Danube (see page 105). This is one of several exceptionally picturesque castles you pass on the **Wachau cruise** from wine-growing **Krems** to **Melk**, whose Benedictine monastery church is one of the world's most magnificent examples of Baroque art.

## Crisp Krems Wine

The train from Wien Franz Josef's Station takes an hour to get to Krems, passing **Klosterneuburg Monastery** perched on its Vienna Woods mountain. Krems is a wealthy 1000-year-old wine town and port made up of three villages: **Krems**, **Stein** and **Und**. The **Piaristenkirche** tower in Krems used to be the town's lookout post in the days of marauding river brigands.

**Above:** *Sailing is a popular summer pastime on Neusiedler See.*

### NOTHING FOR ME?

Some of the yellow postboxes in Austria have the following words written on them: *Haben Sie nichts für mich?* Haven't you got anything for me? Three hundred years ago things were different. In Vienna, for example, mail was delivered six times a day, but the postman ran (not walked or went by bicycle or van) through the city shaking a rattle to tell folk he was coming. He carried a numbered lead box with the mail inside. There were no proper postage stamps then – that had to wait until 1840 for Britain's adhesive Penny Black – so the receiver of the letter paid for its delivery.

### RIDE ON THE WILD SIDE

Bike routes are clearly marked in green Donau-Radwanderweg signs – if you fancy cycling the three hours from Krems to Melk – the best way to see local folk, their villages and sample their wines. For more detailed information, get hold of Rick Steves' annual *Germany, Austria and Switzerland*.

**Stein** is smaller than Krems and does not have the same traffic. The ruins of the **Minoritenkirche** are 13th century and the **Parish Church**, *Pfarrkirche,* has a traditional Baroque onion dome.

From Krems railway station to the Danube cruise embarkation jetty it is a 20-minute walk via a continuity of riverside paths. In the summer there are usually five daily departures to Melk, starting at 10:00.

### Every Hill a Castle

The **cruise boats** are huge three-deck ferries with restaurants, live music, multilingual commentary and snack bars. But, like the fast boats to Budapest, there is no safety drill.

Across a wide river plain opposite Krems is the **Göttweig Benedictine Abbey**, founded in 1083 but rebuilt in 1720, with two onion domes. There are some 18 Benedictine monasteries around Vienna that produce a variety of crops, honey, beer, flowers, wine, grapes and fruit. Nearly all of their wonderful gardens can be visited.

The **Danube** is not very wide in the Wachau valley. It flows swiftly through green, steep-rising, sometimes

**Opposite:** *Pastel-coloured spires like this one at Dürnstein have been much copied, particularly in South America.*
**Right:** *Dürnstein castle and village on the Danube.*

craggy hills of forest and grapevines. It is enormously picturesque, a classic setting for the old medieval *Minnesänger* troubadours who went from castle to castle singing of noble ladies and derring-do in the far-off lands.

## DÜRNSTEIN

For two years Richard the Lionheart was held captive in Dürnstein until the huge ransom Emperor Henry VI demanded was paid. Richard eventually bought his freedom, partly through taxation, in England. The ruins of the castle are on a hill directly above Dürnstein. Dürnstein is only 9km (5m) upriver from Krems. Its baby-blue and white Baroque **church tower** stands dramatically on the riverside on ramparts that look as if they've been there since Richard the Lionheart was forced to disembark.

### NOSTALGIC MOVIES

Films from the old country (*Heimatfilm*) of the 1930s and 1940s, in black and white, have a steady following among more elderly, and perhaps poorer, Viennese. Every afternoon at 16:00, the Bellaria cinema behind the Volkstheater draws in a little crowd to watch Lizzi Waldmüller and Paul Hörbiger's golden oldies from the Ufa or World War II era. The films are scratched, the sound is scratchier but that means nothing to the old dears who sometimes sing quaveringly along with the musical hits.

**Right:** *Melk Monastery's mustard-coloured exterior contains a wealth of Baroque art within.*

As the Danube twists and turns between the hills, the riverbank opens to reveal rolling slopes of vines and two red-capped old churches: **Weissenkirchen** (the white church) and the late Gothic church at Spitz, which also has a navigation museum and some fabulous wines.

In the forested area that comes up further along the river, the 'Venus of Willendorf' was excavated. This 25,000-year-old **fertility statuette** is possibly the oldest (and ugliest) piece of European art ever found. Carved out of limestone, it is now in the prehistoric section of the **Natural History Museum** in Vienna.

## MELK

The giant mustard-yellow **Melk Benedictine Abbey**, first built in 1089, stands high above the Danube and the tiny village that grew at its feet in medieval times. As you look directly up from the little streets of the village, with their ancient historical wall plaques, the façade stretches for 1115m (3695ft).

### OLD MELK TAVERN

You'll see a narrow cobbled lane, restaurant jutting out over the tops of houses below, flowers and a creeper-covered patio. Right below the rock face that soars upward to the walls of Melk Monastery, the Goldener Stern tavern, built in AD1500, transports you back in time. The houses to the left and right announce proudly that one was built in 1390 and another, quotes a writer, in 1230. Two thousand years ago, the Romans built a fort not far from here towards the river which they called Namare.

Dominating the river from every direction, Melk was a Roman 'Limes' or border post 2000 years ago before becoming a pre-Habsburg-dynasty Babenberg fortress and, in 1089, an abbey. It was rebuilt in the early 18th century by local builder Jakob Prandtauer.

## Vision of Paradise

The church's interior was decorated by itinerant Italian masters whose fund of imaginative design was obviously unlimited: rolling wave-topped marble columns, roof roundels and thousands of colourful frescoes adorn every bit of the ceiling. There are balustrades and clouds and angels on the pulpit and on the scrolls of the organ gallery. The walls seem to shiver, blazon and ripple as if revelling in the vast lashings of gilt.

There is nothing real about it at all. It is not meant to be. The idea was to give the congregation an ethereal glimpse of the joys of paradise. The display of wealth, power, art, pomp and glory takes your breath away, and that of the half-million visitors who come here each year. Spirituality is left to a small '**Silent Room**' to the side of the main church with its one candle, one Joseph lily in a glass vase and its unadorned simplicity.

## Monastery for all Seasons

The monastery's long and many-sectioned **Museum** includes an 11th-century portable altar made of walrus horn, and fascinating religious art of the later Middle Ages. Most of **St Koloman's body** lies in Melk Abbey (his head lies in Hungary). He was formerly **Austria's patron saint**, only to be deposed by St Leopold. Melk was occupied on two occasions by the French during the Napoleonic wars. It was a Nazi secondary school in World War II.

The grand **Marble Hall** is linked to the **Library** by an open balcony with expansive views of Melk, the Danube and the surrounding hills. Both Library and Marble Hall have huge and magnificent ceiling frescoes by Paul Troger (1698–1762). There are some 16,000 leather-bound books here, a total of 100,000 in the monastery including 750 'incunabula' or books made

### THE LISTENING EXERCISE

There is a pale blue plaque near the entrance to Melk Monastery. On it, in German and English, is a long quotation from the Brazilian writer Paulo Coelho. It is part of the Jacobsweg pilgrimage route: 'Relax, close your eyes... You will begin to hear voices... They are voices from people of your past, present and future.' There is another of these plaques at the top of town in a little wooded area overlooking Melk and its monastery. Melk is a Slavic word meaning 'slow-moving stream'.

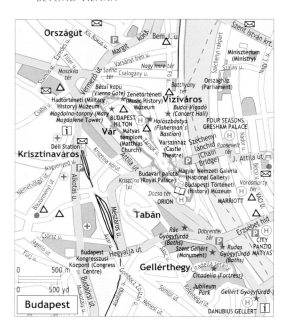

Budapest

prior to the invention of the printing press. The oldest goes back to the 9th century.

The quiet monastery **gardens**, or **Stiftspark**, are a joy to walk through and there is an open-air **restaurant** near the entrance. There is also a **café** in the Baroque **Gartenpavillon** with incredible frescoes of western adventurers and lovely ladies meeting up under giggling conditions with the natives and animals of India, Africa and the Far East. The town of Melk itself, with its turreted houses, cute painted shutters, tiny lanes and family shops, is a delight to stroll through.

## BUDAPEST

The Hungarian people rose up against the Soviet dictatorship in 1956, but in spite of bloody fighting in the streets, with students jumping onto Russian tanks to hurl Molotov cocktails down the hatches, the revolt was brutally put down and former premier **Imre Nagy** executed. It would not be until 1991, after the Berlin Wall was breached and the Soviet Union collapsed, that Hungary would at last be free of Communist domination.

## Statue Park

On the outskirts of the Danube-divided capital of Buda and Pest (pronounced Pesht) is the red-wall-surrounded Statue Park, a circular open museum of the former communist public statues in Budapest. Soviet 'Baroque' is remarkable for its propaganda, naivety, sentimentality and, above all, size. Comrade **Lenin** is here, hand out-stretched, guiding the world forward to scientific social-ism. And of course there is the gallant great-coated **Soviet soldier**, flag in hand, machine gun across his chest. It is part of the 1945 'liberation monument' that was originally downtown on a 7m (22ft) high plinth, in front of a 22m (72ft) tall obelisk and topped by a 13.5m (43ft) figure of a woman with a palm leaf.

The imposing archway into the park is flanked by statues of both **Marx** and **Engels**. There are baked lime-stone monuments to Soviet liberation, memorial stones to the young pioneers (For the worker! For the Homeland! Forward!), several heroic statues to everlast-ing Hungarian-Soviet friendship, and monuments to Hungarian Communists who were 'martyred' defending the Budapest Communist party HQ in the 1956 upris-ing. The most impressive figure is a 9.5m (31ft) bronze

### JEWISH CULTURE

In 1896 Vienna was host to the world's first Jewish, or Jüdisches, Museum closed by the Nazis in 1938. Today's museum in Dorotheergasse is a fascinating celebration of Viennese Jewish culture. Modern, eclectic, its three floors reveal a powerful por-trait of the Jewish contribution to Vienna's artistic, political and medical history and the Jews' relationship down the centuries with a usually hos-tile Gentile populace. Writers Arthur Schnitzler and Josef Roth, composers Arnold Schönberg and Johann Strauss and psychoanalyst Sigmund Freud were all Jewish.

**Left:** *The hydrofoil, or* Schnellboot *(fast boat), flashes past en route to Vienna from Budapest.*

figure of a worker with flag urging his colleagues to the barricades, the most poignant a simple plinth topped by a pair of empty jackboots. With the exception of such countries as North Korea, Zimbabwe and China, there are, worldwide, few Communist dictatorships left today.

### Castles in the Sky

Hungary converted to **Christianity** 1000 years ago. The land was then invaded by Mongols in the 13th century. The Magyar people mixed with the Slavs, Moravians, Germans and Turks. From all this emerged a colourful, dynamic and at times warlike people. But above all they have a fascinating culture, much of which can be seen on Budapest's skyline ridge overlooking the Danube: a series of castles, churches and historical treasures.

Walk across the 130-year-old **Chain Bridge**, or more correctly, Szechényi Bridge in Budapest. Aristocrat Count Szechényi swam across the fierce currents of the Danube to escape from the Soviets after World War II. He and his family settled in Southern Africa. A funicular cable car, built in 1870, takes one up the hill to what is called the **Castle District**.

**Right:** *Pixie spires of the Fishermen's Bastion preen in the Budapest sun.*

**Left:** *Szechényi Bridge across the Danube, looking towards Budapest's Royal Palace.*
**Following page:** *A fiaker hackney cab is a good way of getting around Vienna's old city.*

## Palaces and Parliament

A huge, long building, the Royal Palace, bisected by a cupola, is now a series of museums concentrating on Hungarian art. The **Hungarian National Gallery** has some lovely paintings, not only of the usual royal warriors and statesmen but also more human rural scenes. The palace also houses the country's largest **library**. Entrance is free.

On the right of the palace are the lacy Neo-Gothic spires of the **Matthias Church** and the Neo-Romanesque **Fishermen's Bastion**. The **Gellért Hill Citadel** is the ideal place to take photos. There are some 40 museums and galleries in Budapest.

Other Budapest highlights are the multi-turreted **Parliament** sitting four-square on the Danube, and **St István's Cathedral**, both on the Pest side of the city. The emerald-green and gold-tiled roof of the **Art Museum**, or Iparmúvészeti, is a jewel of Jugendstil art.

Life is more hectic in poorer Budapest than in Vienna: the traffic, the people, the gypsy music, the noise and the rather frenetic rush for business. Possibly the best way to see the city on a short visit is to take a 'Go Local' tour of four to five people led by 'under-guides' who speak a dozen languages.

---

### SPACED OUT

Kàroly Simonyi, who took American citizenship in the 1980s, became the second Kàroly Hungarian space traveller in April 2007. He was presented with the Hungarian Cross of Merit for speaking Hungarian in space. The billionaire Microsoft developer spent a fortnight on board the International Space Station 380km (236 miles) above earth. It cost him US$25 million.

In 1980 Bertalan Farkas, another Hungarian, spent a week in space with a Soviet cosmonaut.

# Vienna at a Glance

April through September.
Unless you plan on skiing, in
which case December
through March. The very best
months are April, May and
September when Vienna is not
so crowded and it is neither
too hot nor too cold. The average amount of rainy days in
any month throughout the
year is eight. The heaviest
rainfall is in June–August.
Vienna is a lot drier than
European capitals further west.
The average day temperature
in May is 19°C (66°F) and in
September 20°C (68°F). In
the hottest summer months
of July–August the temperature
of late has reached in excess of
30°C (86°F).

Non-EU passport holders
should check visa requirements before leaving home.
Citizens of the USA, Canada,
Australia and New Zealand
do not require a visa but
South Africans do. Contact:
Embassy of Austria, 1109
Duncan St, Brooklyn 0181
Pretoria, tel: (012) 4529155.
**By air**: Austrian, tel: (43-1) 05
17 89, www.austrian.com,
tel: (43-1) 7007 22233,
www.viennaairport.com
British Airways, Swiss,
Easyjet, Ryanair, Sky Europe
and others.
**ONLINE BOOKING AGENTS:**
www.cheapflights.co.uk
www.ebookers.com
www.etn.nl/discount

www.lastminute.com
www.opodo.co.uk
www.travelshop.com.au
**By Bus**: Inexpensive daily bus
(22 hours) from London's
Victoria Coach Station. Check
Eurolines Pass, Busabout and
Unlimited Pass for unlimited,
hop-on hop-off, two-week
bus passes in Europe.
**By Rail**: Expensive sleeper-
couper à la Orient Express via
Paris. Cheaper if you take a
six-birth compartment. Don't.
International Rail (UK)
tel: 0870/751 5000,
www.international-rail.com
**By Car**: From London, a day
and a night on the motor-
ways. From, say, Calais it is
1200km (746 miles).
International Driving licence.
Check for essential further
requirements from AA, RAC
or car hire company.
**On arrival**: Valid passport
will enable you to stay for 3
months. Take out insurance
to cover illness or injury.
Vienna airport, Flughafen
Wien-Schwechat, is neat,
small and exceptionally well
run. You can exchange
money, get a meal, hire a car,
book a hotel, and there are
taxi offices in the airport.
(About €25 to town, €35 further out.) The smart CAT (Fly
the Train) costs €9 to town,
departures every 30 minutes.
You can also catch the ordinary S-Bahn train, S7, for only
€3. But until you feel more
confident, splurge and take a
taxi straight to your hotel.

Vienna, one-fifth the size of
London, is a visitor-friendly
city of 1.6 million people. Its
history goes back 2000 years.
Practically everyone speaks
English. It lies on the Danube
River and can be divided into
three main areas: the historical city centre, and fanning
out from this, the western
suburbs and the Vienna
Woods, and finally the
Danube and riverside parks to
the east. The east, which you
pass coming in from the airport, is largely industrial and
with one or two must-see
exceptions can be ignored.
Budapest lies to the east,
Baden to the south and
Danube river cruises,
northwest.
You will likely spend much of
your visit in the ancient city,
Innere Stadt, but if you get
museumed-out there is lots of
forest, river and winelands.
Try not to tick off too many
must-see sites. Relax, walk a
lot, have a coffee, chat to
people and you'll capture the
real flavour of Vienna.

**Walking:** By far the best way
to experience Vienna. There
seems to be a surprise around
every corner in this compact
little city. Keep an eye over
your left shoulder when crossing roads. Do not jaywalk.
Cars will normally give way to
you at a zebra crossing even
when there are no lights.

## Vienna at a Glance

Politeness is a Viennese thing. In this feminist era, the lights are only red and green men.
**Air:** No need, unless you're combining your visit with a skiing holiday in the Austrian Alps.
**Bicycles**: There are 500km (311 miles) of cycle paths in Vienna and 50 city bike stations. It's a national pastime. You can rent them using your credit card whenever you see the sign of the red and yellow cyclist, and at the main railway stations. You can take your bike on the S-Bahn and U-Bahn, but not at rush hours. The fare for the bike is 50% of your normal fare.
**Boat:** DDSG is shorthand for one of those gorgeous German names: *Donaudampfschiff-farhrtsgesellschaft*. These cruise boats on the Danube Canal, one of four arms of the Danube and the one nearest the old city, leave from hectic Schwedenplatz for short trips upriver. You can also do an evening Johann Strauss cruise or if you're Australian, the Spare Ribs Fahrt. There are cruises on the picturesque Wachau section of the Danube to Melk and others to Bratislava, the hydrofoil to Budapest and a 12-day cruise from Amsterdam to Vienna in the summer.
**Bus**: As punctual as the trams, the buses – usually brand-new, and with two concertina-linked compartments, some

seats higher than others – tend to feed the outer suburbs. As with the trams you press a button to open the doors to get in, and another to get out. You will see little logos of, e.g., old folk and pregnant women on the seats near the doors. Be nice and vacate as appropriate.
**Car Parking:** Not easy in the Inner City and is restricted to 1.5 hours inside Gürtel. Flash n' cash or tobacconist for vouchers. But at weekends you can do what you like. Good luck.
**Hackney Cab (*Fiaker*):** You'll see these lovely horse-drawn cabs at Albertina Platz (Museum near Mozart Café), Michaelerplatz (Hofburg entrance), Heldenplatz (Hitler's favourite balcony) and Stephansplatz (Cathedral). The cabs will take you for a ride for a mere €60 for 40 minutes. Hitching is not recommended. But if you want to, hitch in pairs and look out for Autohof truck stops. Mitfahrzentrale, at Josefstadt 8, will put hitchers in touch with drivers who will charge a transport fee. No hitching on motorways in Europe.
**Schnellbahn or S-Bahn:** If you're adventurous and choose to go beyond the Inner City, you may end up on one of these. They have a sort of twin lightning-blue insignia. Cheap and every 15–30 minutes from certain

stations. Some (Weasel) are double deckers and air-conditioned. You will need a non-city ticket on these if you're going further afield. Some U-Bahn, trams, buses and trains run until midnight. Thereafter there are a few night owl buses until all hours.
**Taxi:** Unlike London and New York you can rarely flag one down. They all have meters and are not too expensive; often smart limos. Five minutes and one will be at your hotel. You will find the drivers are from all over Europe, even Persia. Not all speak English. Vienna has a superb public transport system. One ticket, which you buy at little corner 'Tabak' shops or U-Bahn stations, will take you onto any and all types of transport as often as you like for the duration of your ticket (and no-one ever asks to see it). Although, if you get caught without a ticket, you will pay a fine of €65.
**Tram (Strassenbahn)**:
There are 30 tram routes and apart from the U-Bahn, this is the fastest way to get around. On most routes, trams run every 5–10 minutes and all traffic gives way to them. Just clock in your ticket (once only, not every journey) in the little blue box on the tram, or Bim, as they are known locally (after the sound of the bell) and off you go. The trams are red and

cream in colour as they have been since 1897. *Haltestelle* means tram stop; there will be timetables posted there. You press a bell to open the doors at stops. There are special ramps on the more modern buses, trains and U-Bahn for those in wheelchairs. If you are just married or would like to take a group, you can rent a bus or a tram.

**U-Bahn**: There are five colour-coded lines. The U2 (magenta) and U4 (green) circle the Innere Stadt while the U1 (red) and the U3 (orange) cut through it.

**Tickets**: Monthly (€45), weekly (€12.50), three-day (€12). Daily tickets include the Vienna Shopping Card and Twenty-four Hours Vienna. The strip tickets are valid for four and eight days, and can be used by more than one person. Each time you travel you punch it in the blue box. The Vienna Card (three-day) gives you discounts in restaurants and museums. Children aged 15 and below travel for free on weekends and public holidays. Children under six years travel for free at any time. Visitors over 60 (women) and 65 (men) can travel return at 50% (Senioren).

### WHERE TO STAY

The Viennese folk know their city by numbered districts. These can be confusing to visitors. Accommodation

therefore has been divided into landmark areas and popular visitor attractions.

### Old City (Innere Stadt)
#### LUXURY
**Ambassador**,
1010 Wien Kärntnerstrasse 22, tel: (01) 961610, www.ambassador.at
The Opera, Musikverein and Hofburg are only minutes away. Kärntnerstrasse is one of Vienna's most prestigious shopping streets.

**Hotel Bristol**,
1015 Wien, Kärntnerring 1, tel: (01) 515160, www.luxury collection.com/bristol
Built in 1892, lots of original furnishings. Excellent symbiosis of antique elegance and modern hotel technology.

**Hotel Imperial**,
1015 Wien, Kärntnerring 16, tel: (01) 501100, www.luxury collection.com/imperial
A historical palace since 1863, original furnishings. Butler service for suite guests. Impressive list of famous guests, including heads of state. Probably most expensive hotel in Vienna.

**Palais Coburg**,
1010 Wien, Coburgbastei 4, tel: (01) 518180, www.palais-coburg.com
Luxury all-suite hotel in an antique city palace with a modern, luxury touch. There are 35 individually designed suites. Exquisite restaurant with an outstanding selection of wine.

**Hotel Sacher**,
1010 Wien, Philharmonikerstrasse 4, tel: (01) 514560, www.sacher.com
Founded as a hotel in 1876, privately managed since then. One of the most prestigious hotels of Vienna. Relaxing spa refuge. Home of the famous jam-filled dark chocolate Sachertorte.

**Vienna Marriott Hotel**,
1010 Wien, Parkring 12a, tel: (01) 515180, www.viennamarriott.com
Marriott service combined with Viennese hospitality. Has a full range of facilities and is more of a business hotel.

### Old City
#### MID-RANGE
**Austria Trend Hotel Rathaus Park**, 1010 Wien, Rathausstrasse 17, tel: (01) 404120, www.austria-trend.at/rhw
A beautiful *palais* near the new City Hall and Burg Theater. Former residence of Austrian *fin-de-siècle* writer Stefan Zweig (*Letter from an Unknown Woman* and *Beware of Pity*).

**Mailberger Hof**,
1010 Wien, Annagasse 7, tel: (01) 5120641, www.mailbergerhof.at
A very comfortable small family-run hotel in the city centre; situated in a Baroque palace.

## Vienna at a Glance

### Museums Quartier Area
#### MID-RANGE
**Falkensteiner Hotel Am Schottenfeld**,
1070 Wien,
Schottenfeldgasse 74,
www.falkensteiner.com
A young and innovatively designed hotel, not too far from the Volkstheater.

**Arcotel Wimberger**,
1070 Wien, Neubaugürtel 34–36, tel: (01) 521650,
www.arcotel.at
Great diversity of people, artists, globetrotters, business guests. Close to Mariahilferstrasse, Museums Quartier and Spittelberg. Popular for conventions.

#### BUDGET
**Believe It Or Not Hostel**,
1070 Wien, Myrthengasse 10/apt. 14, tel: (01) 5264658,
www.believe-it-or-not-vienna.at
A tiny hostel set in a large private apartment. No groups. Fully equipped kitchen, free internet access, no curfew, cheap beds. The age limit is 17–30 years.

### Schönbrunn Palace Area
#### LUXURY
**Courtyard by Marriott Wien Schönbrunn**,
1120 Wien, Schönbrunner Schlosstrasse 38–40,
tel: (01) 8101717,
A modern hotel next to Schönbrunn Palace. Has comfortable rooms and a mini-gym.

#### MID-RANGE
**Altwienerhof**,
1150 Wien, Herklotzgasse 6,
tel: (01) 892 60 00,
www.altwienerhof.at
Not too far from Westbahnhof station.

**Renaissance Wien Hotel**,
1150 Wien, Linke Wienzeile/Ullmanstrasse 71,
tel: (01) 891020.
Classy hotel with an elegant ambience. Pool and fitness centre.

### Wooded & Green Areas
#### MID-RANGE
**Austria Trend Hotel Schloss Wilhelminenberg**,
1160 Wien, Savoyenstrasse 2,
tel: (01) 4858503,
www.austria-trend.at/wiw
Castle hotel on the western edge of the city. Wonderful view over the city.

**Landhaus Fuhrgassl Huber**,
1190 Wien, Rathsstrasse 24,
tel: (01) 4402714,
www.fuhrgassl-huber.at
Traditional Heuriger, or Viennese wine tavern, located in the vineyards around Neustift am Walde. Quiet, comfortable rooms with stylish ambience.

**Gartenhotel Glanzing**, 1190 Wien, Glanzinggasse 23,
tel: (01) 4704272,
www.gartenhotel-glanzing.at
Charming, four generations family-run hotel. Spring to autumn, the house is overgrown with wild grapevines. Easy public transport access to the city centre.

#### BUDGET
**Hostel Hütteldorf**, 1130 Wien, Schlossberggasse 8,
tel: (01) 8771501. Quiet location en route to Vienna Woods. Free lockers, table tennis and billiards.

### Naschmarkt Area
#### MID-RANGE
**Austria Trend Hotel Ananas**,
1050 Wien, Rechte Wienzeile 93–95,
tel: (01) 546200.
Situated right next to the Naschmarkt and Secession. Good facilities for groups.

**Small Luxury Hotel Das Tyrol**, 1060 Wien, Mariahilferstrasse 15,
tel: (01) 5875415,
www.das-tyrol.at
Trendy boutique hotel on the Mariahilferstrasse, Vienna's longest shopping street.

**Hotel Carlton Opera**, 1040 Wien, Schikanedergasse 4,
tel: (01) 587 53 02,
www.carlton.at
Art Nouveau Jugendstil hotel in a central location.

### Lichtenstein Albertina Area
#### MID-RANGE
**Arcotel Boltzmann**, 1090 Wien, Boltzmanngasse 8,
tel: (01) 316120,
www.arcotel.at/boltzmann
Popular neighbourhood, close to the American embassy.

**Hotel Mozart**, 1090 Wien, Julius-Tandler-Platz 4,
tel: (01) 317 24 77, www.hotel mozart-vienna.at Not far from the Danube Canal.

# Vienna at a Glance

## Belvedere Palace Area
### MID-RANGE
**Hotel Artis Wien**, 1030
Wien, Rennweg 51, tel: (01)
71325210, www.artis.at
A modern and comfortable
city hotel. Some rooms have
water beds.
**NH Belvedere**, 1030 Wien,
Rennweg 12a, tel: (01) 20611,
www.nh-hotels.com
Renovated Art Nouveau
building in a quiet area
surrounded by embassies.
View of the Belvedere Palace
and Botanical Garden.

## Mariahilfer Shopping Area
### BUDGET
**Hostel Ruthensteiner**, 1150
Wien, Robert Hamerling
Gasse 24, tel: (01) 8934202.
Non-smoking hostel close to
Westbahnhof. Free use of the
kitchen and barbeque area.
**Wombat's City Hostel
Vienna**, 1060 Wien,
Mariahilferstrasse 137,
tel: (01) 8972336.
Very clean, free lockers, free
use of the guest kitchen. No
age limit, no curfew.

## Here and There
### MID-RANGE
**Renaissance Penta Vienna
Hotel**, 1030 Wien,
Ungargasse 60, tel: (01)
711750, www.renaissance
hotels.com/VIESE
Hotel from the times of the
monarchy in a former military
riding school. Has a pretty
garden and is not far from
Stadtpark.

**Hotel Stefanie**,
1020 Wien, Taborstrasse 12,
tel: (01) 211500,
www.schick-hotels.com
Traditional hotel, quite near the
Augarten, where the Vienna
Boys' Choir go to school. Has
many years of personal atmosphere and service.

### BUDGET
**Blue Corridor Hostel**, 1070
Wien, Siebensterngasse 15,
tel: (0676) 4919231.
Great location in the hippie
Biedermeier neighbourhood
of Spittelberg. Surrounded by
restaurants and bars. Age limit
of 45 years. Above that, pre-
sumably, one is on the shelf.
**Hotel Cyrus**, 1100 Wien,
Laxenburgerstrasse 14,
tel: (01) 6022578.
Close to the metro,
10 minutes to the city centre.
Free internet access.
**Hotel Geblergasse**, 1170
Wien, Geblergasse 21,
tel: (01) 4063366.
Close to public transport.
Internet access in the rooms.
Twenty-four-hour check-in.
**Westend City Hostel**, 1060
Wien, Fügergasse 3,
tel: (01) 597 67 29.
Rooms with bunk beds, break-
fast, lockers and showers.
Twenty-four-hour reception.

### Apartments
**Appartement Pension 700m
zum Ring**, 1090 Wien,
Van-Swieten-Gasse 8,
tel: (01) 409 36 80,
www.mrhotels.at

Central location not far from
Schottentor station. Great for
families.
**Belvedere Apartments**,
1030 Wien, Fasangasse 18,
tel: (01) 7984499, www.belv.at
Serviced apartments for one
to six persons next to
Belvedere Palace and
Gardens.
Price ranges: €18–25 and
above; €12–18; €12 and €12
and below. (US$1 = €0.74,
approximately.)
**Mondial Appartement Hotel**,
1090 Wien, Alserbachstrasse/
Pfluggasse 1, tel: (01) 3107180,
www.mondial.at
Sixteen apartments, each
with its own individual
character, partly furnished
with antiques. Situated near
the old city.

### WHERE TO EAT

**DO&CO Albertina**, 1010
Wien, Albertinaplatz 1.
Back of the opera,
tel: (01) 5329669. Seats
indoors 50, outdoors 60.
Open daily 09:00–24:00.
Over €25. Austrian, Asian
and Mediterranean food.
Breakfast in the morning,
snacks 15:00–18:00. Great
bar with panoramic views.
**Fabio's**, 1010 Wien,
Tuchlauben 4–6, tel: (01) 532
22 22, seats 120. Mon–Sat
10:00–01:00. Over €18–25.
Fairly pricey top-notch Italian
restaurant. Popular with locals.
**Harry's Time**, 1010 Wien,
Dr. Karl Lueger-Platz 5.
Tel: (01) 5124556.

# Vienna at a Glance

Open Mon–Fri 10:00–01:00, Sat 18:00–24:00. Cost: €18–25. Creative and diverse dishes. Black and white décor. Popular with young people employed in the nearby banks and offices.
**Livingstone**, 1010 Wien, Zelinkagasse 4, tel: (01) 5333393-15. Seats indoors 130, outdoors 80. Open daily 17:00–04:00. Cost: €12–18. Great steaks and seafood. Palms, wood and colonial ambience. Food is prepared until 03:30 in the morning.
**Mörwald im Ambassador**, 1010 Wien, Kärntnerstrasse 22, tel: (01) 96161161. Seats indoors 80, outdoors 12. Open daily 11:00–15:00, 18:00–23:00. Cost: €25. Expensive, famous and good classic European cuisine.
**Regina Margherita**, 1010 Wien, Palais Esterházy, Wallnerstrasse 4, tel: (01) 5330812. Open daily 12:00–15:00 and 18:00–24:00. Cost: €12–18. A very conservative pizzeria in the heart of the city. Served in a beautiful outdoor dining area in the courtyard of Palais Esterházy.
**Sky Restaurant**, 1010 Wien, Kärntnerstrasse 19, tel: (01) 5131712. Seats 200. Open Mon–Sat 18:00–01:00. Cost: €18–25. Open as a café 10:30–18:00. Everyone's favourite view of Vienna city.
**Yohm**, 1010 Wien, Petersplatz 3, tel: (01) 5332900. Seats 40.

Open daily 12:00–15:00 and 18:00–24:00. Cost: €18–25. Asian restaurant east of Kathmandu. All sorts of dishes, especially fish. Not far from Stephansdom City Centre.
**Zum Schwarzen Kameel**, 1010 Wien, Bognergasse 5, tel (01) 5338125. Seats 75. Open Mon–Sat 08:30–24:00. Cost: €18–25. Family-run restaurant in the heart of the old city. Traditional Viennese cuisine as well as snacks. Look for the black camel sign going back to 1618.
**Café Hummel**, 1080 Wien, Josefstädterstrasse 66, tel: (01) 405 53 14. Seats 120. Open Mon–Sat 07:00–24:00, Sun 08:00–24:00. Cost: €12–18. Watch local folk play chess and cards in this traditional café. Family-run since 1937.
**Café Landtmann**, 1010 Wien, Dr. Karl Lueger-Ring, tel: (01) 241000. Seats indoors 380, outdoors 350. Open daily 07:30–24:00. Cost: €12–18. Elegant coffee house near the Burgtheater, founded in 1873. All the traditional Viennese coffee specialities and dishes. Sigmund Freud, Marlene Dietrich, and Paul McCartney have all eaten here.
**EF16**, 1010 Wien, Fleischmarkt 16, tel: (01) 513 23 18. Seats 60. Open Mon–Fri 11:30–15:00, Mon–Sat 17:30–23:00. Cost: €12–18.

A new restaurant with 400-year-old arches. Has a Northern Italian 'Osteria' style. Mixture of Italian and Viennese specialties.
**Gastwirtschaft Huth**, 1010 Wien, Schellinggasse 5, tel: (01) 5135644. Seats 60. Open daily 11:30–24:00. Cost: €12–17. A 'noble' Viennese *Beisl* serving traditional as well as creative new Viennese cuisine.
**Lusthaus**, 1020 Wien Freudenau 254/at the end of Prater Hauptallee, tel: (01) 7289565. Open May–Sep: Thu–Tue 12:00–23:00, but Sat–Sun 12:00–18:00, Wed closed. Oct–Apr: daily 12:00–18:00. Cost: €12–18. Surrounded by the Prater's huge recreational area across the Danube. Very romantic. Nice terrace.
**Más**, 1080 Wien, Laudongasse 36, tel: (01) 4038324. Seats 120. Mon–Wed & Sun 18:00–24:00, Thu–Sat 18:00–01:00. Cost: €12–18. Trendy restaurant with lots of young locals. Cocktail bar, good Latin-American dishes. Have some tapas.
**Meixner's Gastwirtschaft**, 1100 Wien, Buchengasse 64, tel: (01) 604 27 10. Seats indoors 120, outdoors 45. Open daily 11:30–22:00. Cost: €12–18. Classic Viennese cuisine with seasonal specialities. Beautiful garden.

# Vienna at a Glance

**Naschmarkt**, U4 station Karlsplatz or Kettenbrückengasse. Open 06:00–22:00. Cost: €2–15, Vienna's most lively market. Tiny restaurants: traditional Austrian cuisine, Balkans, Far East – anything from Palatschinken to seafood, kebab and wok. Vienna – a multicultural melting pot.

**Palmenhaus im Burggarten**, 1010 Wien, Burggarten, entrance at the Albertina, tel: (01) 5331033.
Seats indoors 130, outdoors 250. Open daily 10:00–02:00. Cost: €12–18.
A restaurant in a Victorian station-like palm house (a former botanical garden). Few but creative dishes. Outdoor terrace. There is a tropical butterfly house next door.

**Wolf**, 1070 Wien, Burggasse 76. tel (01) 9906620.
Cost: €12–18.
Combination of a traditional Viennese *Beisl* (pub) and a trendy, modern restaurant. Marvellous Viennese cuisine and a fine selection of wines.

**Zur Alten Kaisermühle**, 1220 Wien, Fischerstrand 21A, tel: (01) 2633529. Seats 120. Open daily 11:30–23:00. Cost: €12–18.
Right on the Danube before Kagraner Bridge.

**Beim Cumpelik**, 1080 Wien, Buchfeldgasse 10. tel: (01) 4032520. Seats 75. Open Mon–Sat 11:00–14:30, 17:30–23:00. Cost: €8–12.

Friendly, rustic *Beisl* in the centre of a Biedermeier neighbourhood in the 8th district. Traditional Viennese cuisine.

**Blaustern**, 1190 Wien, Döblinger Gürtel 2, tel: (01) 3696564. Seats indoors 130, outdoors 90. Open Mon–Fri 07:00–01:00, Sat–Sun 08:00–02:00. Cost: €8–12.
A pleasant café and restaurant, popular with students from the nearby university. Good breakfasts.

**Brückenwirt**, 1100 Wien, Unterlaaerstrasse 27, tel: (01) 688 38 83.
Cost: €12 and below.
Rustic, friendly pub on the outskirts of Vienna. Traditional Viennese cuisine served in huge portions.

**Café Stein**, 1090 Wien, Währingerstrasse 6–8, tel: (01) 3197241. Open Mon–Sat 07:00–01:00. Cost: €8–12.
Famous Viennese café close to the old university on the Ringstrasse. Cosy ambience.

**Centimeter I**, 1080 Wien, Lenaugasse 11, tel: (01) 470060641. Seats 120. Open Mon–Fri 10:00–24:00, Sat–Sun 11:00–01:00. Cost: €6–8.
Creative restaurant chain, order sandwiches by centimeters. There is also a huge variety of beers. Groups can choose to share one huge dish. Wheel barrow or Sword are popular favourites.

**Glacisbeisl**, 1070 Wien, Museums Quartier, Zugang Breite Gasse 4, tel: (01) 5265660. Open daily 11:00–02:00. Cost: €8–12.
Trendily designed *Beisl* inside Museums Quartier. Traditional Viennese cuisine with a modern interpretation.

**Kopp**, 1200 Wien, Donaueschingenstrasse 28, tel: (01) 3328082. Seats 100. Open daily 06:00–02:00. Cost: €15 and under.
Viennese specialities, huge portions, reasonable prices.

**Plachutta Hietzing**, 1130 Wien, Auhofstrasse 1, tel: (01) 877 70 87. Seats 100. Cost: €15 and under.
The Plachutta family restaurants (there is also one in the 1st district and one in the 19th) are famous for their Viennese beef dishes. Be sure to taste the 'Tafelspitz' boiled fillet of beef.

**Nells Gastwirtschaft**, 1180 Wien, Alseggerstrasse 26, tel: (01) 4791377. Seats indoors 130, outdoors 80. Cost: €8–12. Between Währing and Gertshof districts in the western suburbs.

**Oktagon**, 1190 Wien, Himmelstrasse Ecke Höhenstrasse, tel: (01) 328 89 36. Open Wed–Fri 12:00–22:00, Sat–Sun 11:00–22:00. Cost: €12 and under.
Remote Wienerwald, ideal place to relax after a walk in the Vienna woods. Incredible views over Vienna.

## Vienna at a Glance

**Rudi's Beisl**, 1050 Wien, Wiedner Hauptstrasse 88, tel: (01) 544 51 02. Seats 30. Open Mon–Fri 11:00–15:00, 18:00–23:00. Cost: €15 and under. Tiny little *Beisl* serving Viennese cuisine at its best. Reservation required.

**Salettl Pavillon**, 1190 Wien, Hartäckerstrasse 80, tel: (01) 4792222. Seats indoors 50, outdoors 250. Open daily 06:30–01:00. Cost: €8–12. Frequented mostly by locals from the surrounding area. Very romantic. Try the ham-and-cheese croissant.

**Wrenkh**, 1010 Wien, Bauernmarkt 10, tel: (01) 5331526. Open Mon–Sat 11:30–23:00. Cost: €8–12. Tiny restaurant in the city centre. Specialises in vegetarian dishes but also meat and fish. The organic fruit juices are freshly prepared.

**Zu den 2 Lieserln**, 1070 Wien, Burggasse 63, tel: (01) 5233282. Open daily 11:00–23:00. Cost: €8–12. Actually a sight in itself. The Viennese have been eating Schnitzel and roasts here since the days of Marshal Radetzky, who crushed the 1848 revolution. Try the onion and vanilla roast.

AUTHOR'S SUGGESTIONS:
**Weingut Mayer** on Pfarrplatz. Pfarrplatz 2, tel: (01) 370 3361. Seats 200. Open daily 16:00–24:00 except Sun 11:00–24:00. Cost: €12–18. Heuriger wine farm, inner courtyard, not far from Grinzing in an old farmhouse where Beethoven once lived. The new wine is the one to taste e.g. Grüner Veltliner.

**Die Wirtschaft**, Pötzleinsdorferstrasse 67, tel: (01) 479 2857. Seats 84. Open daily except Sun and Mon 11:00–24:00. Cost: €12 and under. Viennese pub and garden, personally run by owner Barbara Bonka who also has a restaurant in the Vienna Woods. Take Tram 41 to the end of the line.

**Ilona Stuberl**, Bräunerstrasse 2, Innere Stadt, tel: (01) 533 90 29. Seats 50. Cost: €12–18. Open every day 11:30–23:30 1 Apr to 30 Sep. Rest of the year, closed on Mon. Small Hungarian restaurant off the Graben. Try the prune soup with almonds, and fried carp.

**Café Central**, I, Herrengasse 14, tel: (01) 533 6763. Seats 150. Open 07:30–22:00 and Sun 10:00–18:00. A coffee costs €3.50. You wait at the door, a smart jacketed waiter will take your coat, world newspapers available. The ceiling is neo-Gothic, a pianist plays light music.

### SHOPPING

ANTIQUES:
**Das Kunstwerk**, 4 Operngasse 20. Open 11:00–18:00. Art Deco, Jugendstil by Austrian designers Otto Wagner, Adolf Loos, Thonet and Kohn (U-Bahn 2, Karlsplatz).

BOOKS:
**Shakespeare & Co**, I, Sterngasse 2. Excellent English language bookstore but no sleeping alcoves for impoverished writers as in the Shakespeare in Paris. (U-Bahn 4 Schwedenplatz.)

BARGAINS:
**Naschmarkt flea-market** for second-hand goods and haggling fun. (U2 Karlsplatz.)

CAMERAS AND FILM DEVELOPING:
Try any of many branches of Niedermeyer (e.g. U2 Schottentor).

COMPUTERS (FIXING):
Der Computer Doctor, 18, Gentzgasse 9. (U-6 Volksoper.)

CLOTHES:
**Innere Stadt**
Has all the top designer-label stores along Graben and Kohlmarkt (U3 Stephansplatz).
**Department Stores**
Steffl, I, Kärntnerstrasse 19, (U3 Stephansplatz).
Also good value:
Woolworths, Schlosshoferstrasse 3–5, Floridsdorf (U6 Floridsdorf).

FOOD:
Try any of many branches of Spar Gourmet.
Also, Meinl am Graben's elegant grocery (U1 Stephansplatz).

# Vienna at a Glance

**JEWELLERY:**
There are so many jewellery shops to choose from. Köchert were jewellers to the Imperial Court. I, Neuer Markt 15 (U1 Stephansplatz).

**PORCELAIN:**
Augarten – second oldest in Europe. Showroom of hand-finished and painted porce-lain (U1 Nestroyplatz).

**CHOCOLATES:**
Truffles at Café Central choc shop, round the corner from the Café (U2 Schottentor). There are superb – and expensive – chocolate shops anywhere.

**WINE:**
Wein & Co chain. Try the one (and the deli) near the Naschmarkt. Open daily until 24:00 (U2, U4, Karlsplatz).

**HEALTH & BEAUTY:**
Bipa is a chain selling cos-metic products.

**TOURS AND EXCURSIONS**

If you are not familiar with the internet, try: **Ina Deinhammer TUI-Blaguss Travel**, Obkirchergasse 17, tel: (43 1) or in Vienna (01) 369 40 36, e-mail: IDeinhammer@ blaguss.at Your hotel may help you with opera and tour book-ings and detailed destination printouts of how to get there. City Bus Tours, try **Vienna Sightseeing Tours**, tel: (01) 7124 6830, www. viennasightseeingtours.com You can combine these tours with Vienna Boys' Choir and Spanish Riding School.
**Danube Boat Trips:** DDSG at Schwedenplatz, www.ddsg-blue-danube.at You can take short river trips or longer to Bratislava and Budapest.
**Music Mile Vienna:**
For western classical music fans, tel: (01) 58830-0. www.musikmeile.at
**Architecture:** Old and new for building buffs, www.azw.at (Architekturzentrum Wien).

**Third Man Tour:** Possibly the best tour of all. By metro U-Bahn to the many locations of post World War II Vienna where the iconic 1949 film *Der Dritte Mann* was filmed. Wien-Tourismus, tel: (01) 774 8901, e-mail: info@viennawalks.com Tours approx. every 4 days.
**Walking Tours:** Vienna Walks & Talks, tel: (01) 774 8901, www.vienna walks.tix.at

**USEFUL CONTACTS**

**Police**: tel: 133, **Fire**: tel: 122
**Ambulance**: tel: 144
**Auto accident emergencies**: tel: 120
**Flight information**: tel: 7007 22233
www.viennaairport.com
**Bus / Tram**: U-Bahn, tel: 7909 105, www.wienerlinien.at
**Embassies:**
**British Consulate**, tel: 7161 35151; **South African Em-bassy**, tel: 3206 4930; **US Embassy**, tel: 31399; **Aus-tralian Embassy**, tel: 50674.

# Travel Tips

## Tourist Information

**Austrian Tourist Office:**
They have a range of brochures and information on practically any query. Margaretenstrasse 1 (U4 to Margaretengürtel), tel: (01) 588 660 or 0810 101818, www.austria.info
Closed at weekends.

**Vienna Tourist Office:** Not as good or multilingual as the above. No. 1 Albertinaplatz/ Maysedergasse, tel: (01) 24 555 (U2 Karlsplatz), www.vienna.info
Open 09:00–19:00 daily.

## General Information

For booking hotels, car rental etc, see www.tiscover.com

## Entry Requirements

EU citizens require only a valid national identity card. Everyone else, including UK, needs a passport. No visas required for Australian, British Canadian, New Zealand and US citizens. South Africans need a visa.

## Customs

Bring in as much as you like if the items were purchased in another EU country. But if you are coming from a non-EU country or the goods were purchased in a duty-free, much lower limits apply, e.g. 200 cigarettes, one litre of spirits. Uncooked meat, weapons, drugs, dairy products, animal skins, and so on may get you into trouble with the customs officers.

## Health

There are no special requirements for entry into Vienna unless you are coming from endemic disease areas (check with your travel agent or nearest Austrian embassy). Austria has a superb health care system. Having an EU or British passport ensures free health care. Take out medical insurance, however; the free health variety involves much form-filling. Serious illnesses will always be treated quickly and money concerns discussed later.

## Getting There

See page 113.

## What to Pack

Vienna can be very hot in summer and very cold with an icy wind in winter. You can buy anything locally, of course, but shorts, sandals, sun cream, shades and hat for summer are advisable. Summer is also the highest rainfall season, so bring an umbrella. A good pair of walking boots will be useful for the many parks and Vienna Woods. Bring jacket and tie for the opera. For winter visitors, dress as you would for any country where it snows. A Swiss knife (in hold luggage) is always handy. And a novel.

## Money Matters

**Currency:** Euro banknotes come in the following denominations: 5, 10, 20 50, 100, 200 and 500. Always carry a 50 cent coin on you for the WC. Banks are open 08:00–12:30 and 13:30–15:00.

**Exchange Rates:**
The Euro is stable and does not change much. Roughly €1.50 to the pound and €0.75 to the US$. Travellers cheques are not as useful as ATM credit cards.

*Wechselstube,* or exchange booths, that accept major currencies are available in the city.

### ATMs and Credit Cards
Widely available and widely used. But credit cards not so widely used (shops and restaurants) as, e.g, in UK and USA.

## Accommodation
Reserve your hotel (on the web) before you arrive, at least for the first three nights. There is every type of hotel, wine farm, apartment and backpackers lodge available. Hotels will often negotiate if you are staying a while but not necessarily in the high summer season. Continental breakfast usually comes with the room.

## Eating Out
Eating out is the Vienna thing to do. There are some 2000 restaurants, cafés, pubs and bars. Apart from Viennese specialities (especially cakes and coffee and 'slices', or *schnitzels*), there are Japanese, Chinese (lots), Indian, Thai, Greek, Italian (lots), Balkan, American (burgers), French, Israeli, Hungarian, Russian, Tibetan, Brazilian, Levantine, Korean. The lot. No need to dress up but you will feel out of place in trainers and T-shirt in the smarter restaurants. Vienna cuisine concentrates on meats (try boar) but fish from the Danube is good. And you must try a fast-food *wurst*, mustard and roll at any of a hundred corner stands.

## Transport
*See* Getting There (page 113) and Getting Around (pages 113–115).

## Business Hours
All shops, except bakeries, are closed on Sundays. And many smaller ones close for lunch. Hours are: 08:00 or 09:00 to about 18:00. Some museums stay open with free entrance. School summer holidays are in July–August. Quite a few galleries and theatres close for part of the time, otherwise they are open Tuesday–Sunday, 10:00–18:00. Churches (many with fabulous interiors) are open 07:00–19:00 but in quite a few you can only get into the grilled foyer.

## Time
Vienna time is GMT plus one hour in summer and plus two hours in winter.

## Communications
**Telephones**: The international dialling code for Vienna is +431 or 00431. Phone booths have instructions in four languages. Note: numbers ending in 0, no need to dial the final 0. This final 0 means it's a line with direct dial extensions. Phone cards are more common than cash at booths. Buy them at any Tabak, Trafik or post office. A telephone charge card from home, using a pin number, is convenient. Directory enquiries: 118877. Mobile: 0800 664 664.
**Mobiles**: Known as 'handy' in Vienna. Everyone seems to

have one and to spend a good deal of time thereon. Check with your mobile service provider before leaving home to see if your package will function in Vienna – unless you have a tri-band phone.
**Internet Cafés:** There are plenty. In addition, restaurants and cafés – in keeping with the Viennese tradition of free newspaper reading – will allow you access. The AOL access number from Vienna is 585 8483, Compuserve 0049-180 570 40 70, and EUnet is 899 330.
**Post:** Look up *Post und Telegraphenverwaltung* for the post office nearest to you. The postal service is excellent, staff usually English-speaking. There are post offices at the three main railway stations. The main post

### HIGH SEASON AND HOLIDAYS

**1 Jan** • New Year
**6 Jan** • Epiphany
Easter Monday (major holiday weekend)
**1 May** • Labour day
**6th Thursday after Easter** • Ascension Day
**6th Monday after Easter** • Whit Monday
**2nd Thursday after Whitsuntide** • Corpus Christi
**15 August** • Assumption Day
**1 November** • All Saints Day (thousands visit cemeteries)
**26 October** • Austria National Day
**25 December** • Christmas Day, *Weihnachtstag*
**26 December** • 'Boxing Day' or St Stephen's Day

office is at 1 Fleischmarkt not far from Schwedenplatz, U-Bahn U1 or U4. Open daily from 06:00–22:00.

## Electricity

220V which is quite acceptable for, e.g., British 240V appliances. Bring an adaptor (plugs have 2 pins) and transformer if you have 110V equipment.

## Weights and Measures

Vienna uses the metric system.

## Health Precautions

Most visitors drink water in blue bottles but the Vienna tap water is perfectly safe and tasty. Vienna is a café culture society, so tainted food is exceptionally rare. If you get travel diarrhoea, the nearest Apotheke will advise you to drink diluted cola and eat as little as possible. Take out medical cover insurance. Pharmacies usually require a doctor's prescription. If you want to be 100% reassured, contact Medical Advisory Service to Travellers Abroad (www.masta.org).

## Medical Emergencies

**Ambulance** tel: 144
**Auto Accident** tel: 120
**Vienna Medical Association Service** (foreign patients), 1, Weihburggasse 10–12, tel: 5150 1213 or 24/7 hotline 5139595 (U3, U1 Stephansplatz). The actual office is manned and open 08:00–16:00 Mon–Wed and 08:00–18:00 Thu, and 08:00–14:00 Fri. Aids testing in Vienna can be done at AIDS-Hilfe Wien, 6, Mariahilfer Gürtel 4 (U6 Gumpendorfer), tel: 599370.

**Children's Hospital** (Sankt Anna Kinderspital), 9, Kinderspitalgasse 6, tel: 401700 (U6 Alser Strasse). Doctors are on duty 24 hours a day.

**Emergency Ward** Hospital Allgemeines Krankenhaus (AKH). Largest hospital in Europe. 9, Wärhinger Gürtel 18–20, tel: 40 400-0.

**Alcoholics Anonymous** tel: 799 5599.

Note: For visitors who have been to India, Africa or South America, this may sound

paranoid. But in the Vienna Woods you should beware of ticks which can, rarely, cause Central European encephalitis (CEE). Dress as you would in Africa, in hat, long trousers and long-sleeved shirt. Pull the tick off but if itchiness or fever results, see a doctor.

## Personal Safety

The only problem you may meet is a skateboarder narrowly missing you on the steps of either the Burgtheater or Belvedere Palace.

Vienna is a particularly safe city and the Viennese are famous for being law-abiding. The Gürtel ring roads are reputedly a bit red-lightish and the Karlsplatz underground station a dope and punch-up booze area, Südbahnhof and Stadtpark should perhaps be avoided after dark, and Schwedenplatz can be hectic.

Wearing a money belt pouch immediately identifies you as a foreigner anywhere in the world – but it is highly unlikely you'll meet a bag-snatcher. Carry a photocopy of your I.D. or passport with you. The police are armed but seldom use their weapons – yet they love racing, TV-style, sirens blazing, through the city. You will hardly ever see anyone get angry: it's not the Viennese thing to do.

## CONVERSION CHART

| FROM | TO | MULTIPLY BY |
|------|-----|-------------|
| Millimetres | Inches | 0.0394 |
| Metres | Yards | 1.0936 |
| Metres | Feet | 3.281 |
| Kilometres | Miles | 0.6214 |
| Square kilometres | Square miles | 0.386 |
| Hectares | Acres | 2.471 |
| Litres | Pints | 1.760 |
| Kilograms | Pounds | 2.205 |
| Tonnes | Tons | 0.984 |

To convert Celsius to Fahrenheit: x 9 ÷ 5 + 32

## Useful Phrases

Actually they are not that useful as you are likely to get out of your depth if someone thinks you speak German. However, they do break the ice. Rather get a small pocket dictionary which you can use to identify individual words on shops and notices and street signs. And guess the rest.

## Road signs

The usual international road signs are used in Vienna. The round-city motorways are hectic. Be more careful at no-lights zebra crossings, especially of cars turning corners (they usually do so before you are very far into the crossing, which is allowed). But you will find that Vienna is pedestrian-friendly and the driving non-aggressive.

## Emergencies

*See* Useful Contacts.

## Etiquette

Always try to speak a few (humble) words of German. Vienna is not a big city but it is one with a proud history. The Viennese have a reputation for being reserved, but that soon melts into smiles and helpfulness. The Viennese know well that tourists are important to them. Headwaiters can be stiff-lipped – but that's a traditional act. There is no need to push 'n' shove anywhere. You can wear what you like but be reasonably dress-respectful in churches (there are no decency guardians as in Rome) remembering that the

Viennese are more Catholic-religious than most of Europe. Jacket and tie for the opera but even there you won't be thrown out. Just embarrassed.

## Language

Viennese speak German but with many local *Wienerisch* colloquialisms that incorporate Yiddish, Hungarian and Czech words (their 19th-century empire once incorporated these countries, and many more). Always start with *Grüss Gott* (God's greetings) wherever you are and with everybody. Except perhaps in some taxis, suburbs and countryside, everyone seems to speak English.

## Toilets

The 300-plus public toilets in Vienna are marked WC. Not all are open 24/7. Keep a 50 cent coin on you. Toilets are much rarer in the suburbs. U-Bahn stations usually have toilets. Most cafés will allow you to use their toilet even if you're not a guest.

## Special Interest Groups
### Tips for the Disabled

The Austrian Tourist Board has a leaflet 'Vienna for Visitors with Disabilities', www.austria.info
The Vienna Tourist Office Albertinaplatz/Maysedergasse tel: (01) 24 555, is open daily 09:00–19:00. It has booklets, e.g., on hotels for the disabled plus a disabled booking service. Some sidewalks – but not all public transport – are at street level. Some buses

have fold-out ramps. The old historic trams are not good for the disabled. Guiding stripes on the Underground indicate the exit, elevator and escalator options for folk in wheelchairs. Wiener Linien, tel: (01) 7909-0 have U-Bahn and rail station maps in Braille. The following database www.you-too.net will give you a good idea about the accessibility of public places in Vienna. Being an old city, quite a few of Vienna's many attractions are in historic buildings that are not always access-friendly. There are special guided tours; try www.info.wien.at

## Children
Vienna is of course very child-friendly. And there are attractions specifically for them, including the Puppet Theatre in Schönbrunn, the Technical Museum's adventure area, the funfair and giant Ferris wheel at Prater, the Schönbrunn zoo (and maze), ZOOM Children's Museum and Haus des Meeres (sharks, snakes and piranhas in a former Nazi flak tower aquarium). Schönbrunn Palace has special tours for children (cakes being made for the royal children), the Butterfly House (Schmetterlinghaus) in the Burggarten's Greenhouse and finally an adventure swimming pool (Dianabad Tropicana) with Pirates of the Caribbean and waterslide.

## Student Travellers
There are nine youth hostels in Vienna. You will need an International Youth Hostel Federation members card which you can get at the hostels. In the high season 1 July to 30 September, the hostels tend to revert to being busy hotels. Try the Austrian Youth Hostel Association, Schottenring 28, tel: (01) 533 5353. If you are an EU citizen

you can work in Vienna, so if your German is good, give it a go. The Club International Universitaire (CIU), www.ciu.at, and tel: (01) 533 6533, gives advice to foreign students. Apart from the University of Vienna's 9- and 12-week inexpensive German language courses, www.univie.ac.at/wihok, there are at least 5 other language institutions giving intensive German courses (2–3 weeks).

## Gay and Lesbian Travellers
The Regenbogenparade (Rainbow Parade) takes place in Vienna on the last Saturday in June, www.pride.at The Naschmarkt likes to think of itself as home to the gay district. There are some 8 gay and lesbian nightspots and

the Rosa–Lila Villa flies the rainbow flag. Frauen Café at 8, Langegasse, II (U2 Lerchenfelderstrasse, Josefstadt) is strictly for women. If straight folks in Vienna have hang-ups about sexuality, they don't let on.

## Women Travellers
No special problems. Half the City Council are women. Men may be macho up in the mountains, but they have learned to be good boys in Vienna.

## Senior Travellers
Women over 60 and men over 65 can sometimes get cheaper tickets on all Vienna's transport. Try the Senioren-Servicetelefon, tel: 4000 8580, for options available, plus leisure and cultural activities.

---

### GOOD READING

- **Bachmann**, **Ingeborg**, *Songs in Flight*. Bilingual edition of poems.
- **Clare**, **George**, *Last Waltz in Vienna*. The destruction of a family 1842–1942.
- **Gainham**, **Sarah**, *Night Falls on the City*. Jewish wartime Vienna.
- **Gay**, **Peter**, *Mozart*. Easy-to-read Mozart biography.
- **Greene**, **Graham**, *The Third Man*. Bombed Vienna and black market intrigue.
- **Hamann**, **Brigitte**, *Hitler's Vienna*. Where the dictator picked up most of his violent prejudices.
- **Höpler**, **Vogel et al**, *Vienna City Guide for Children*.
- **Jelinek**, **Elfriede**, *The Piano Teacher*. The novelist was awarded the 2004 Nobel Prize for Literature.
- **Kerr**, **Philip**, *A German Requiem*. Spooks in postwar Vienna.
- **Roth**, **Joseph**, *Radetzky March*. Nineteenth-century Vienna.
- **Zweig**, **Stefan**, *The Burning Secret and Other Stories*. Delicious tales of *fin-de-siècle* Vienna.
- **Rubenfeld**, **Jed**, *The Interpretation of Murder*. A novel.
- **Silva**, **Daniel**, *A Death in Vienna*. A thriller.